Essential Music Theory © 2023 by San Marco Publications. All rights reserved.

All right reserved. No part of this book may be reproduced in any form or by electronic or mechanical means including Information storage and retrieval systems without permission in writing from the author.

ISNB: 9781896499287

Contents

Lesson 1: **Notation**	1
Lesson 2: **Rhythm and Meter**	7
Lesson 3: **Major Scales**	22
Lesson 4: **History 1**	28
Review 1	30
Lesson 5: **Minor Scales**	34
Lesson 6: **Intervals**	45
Lesson 7: **Chords**	54
Lesson 8: **History 2**	59
Review 2	61
Lesson 9: **Melody Writing**	65
Lesson 10: **Music Analysis**	70
Lesson 11: **History 3**	76
Review 3	79
Music Terms and Signs	83

1
Notation

Accidental Review

Study the following accidentals:

    The **sharp** (♯) raises a note one half step
    The **flat** (♭) lowers a note one half step
    The **natural** (♮) cancels the effect of a sharp or flat.

Figure 1.1 shows how accidentals are used in a musical score.

    a) An accidental lasts until the end of the measure.
    b) A bar line cancels an accidental.
    c) When a note has the same letter name but a different pitch, the accidental is written again.
    d) An accidental when tied over the barline is not written again.
    e) An accidental is written again after a tie in the same measure.

Figure 1.1

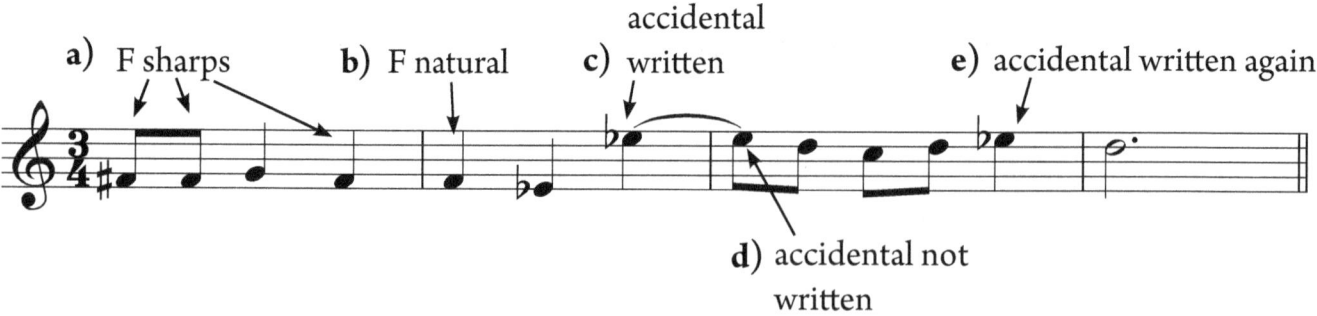

Enharmonic Notes

Each black key on the keyboard has both a sharp name and a flat name. When notes have the same pitch but different names they are said to be *enharmonic equivalents*. Enharmonic really means "same note, different name". They are the same note but they have different meanings. It's like the words there, their, and they're. They sound the same but mean something different. There are very good reasons why we use different names for notes and we will learn about that when we study scales and keys.

Figure 1.2 shows some of the enharmonic notes on the keyboard. Enharmonic notes don't just apply to black keys. Some of the white keys may have more than one name. B♯ is also C and B is also C♭. E♯ is also F and E is also F♭.

Figure 1.2

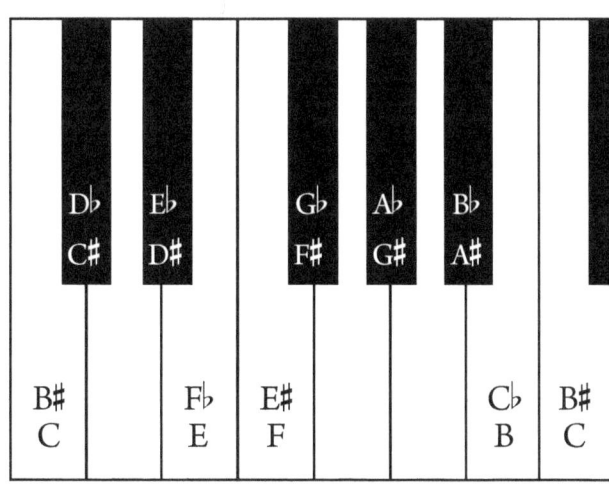

1. Give the enharmonic equivalents for the following notes.

F♯ _____   A♯ _____   F _____

B♭ _____   B _____   G♭ _____

C♯ _____   G♯ _____   D♭ _____

D♯ _____   C _____   A♭ _____

E♯ _____   B♭ _____   E♭ _____

2. In the empty measures write the enhamonic equivalent of the previous notes. Name each note.

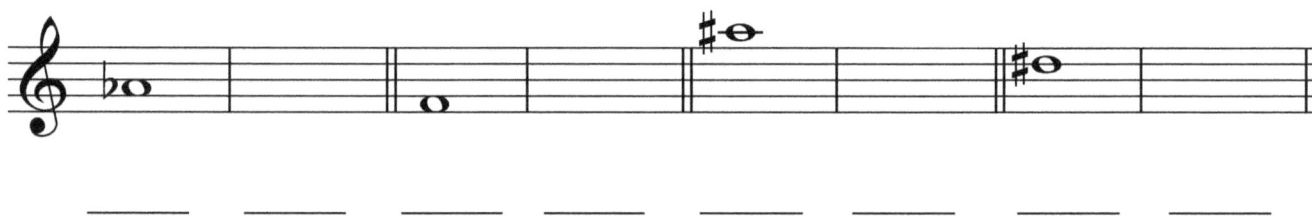

Review - Stem Direction and Beams

Eighth and sixteenth notes are grouped together with beams. When we beam these notes sometimes one or more of the stems are placed differently than would be the case if flags were used. If most of the notes are above the third (middle) line of the staff, stems go downward (Figure 2.6 a). If most of the notes are below the third line, the stems go upward (Figure 2.6 b). Here, majority rules.

Figure 2.6

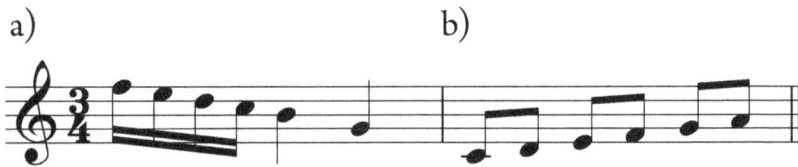

If the number of notes above the middle line of the staff is equal to the number below, the stem direction is determined by the note which is the farthest from the middle line (Figure 2.7).

Figure 2.7

1. Connect each group of four sixteenth notes with stems and beams.

Octave Transposition

An octopus has 8 legs. An octagon has 8 sides. We know from studying intervals than an *octave* is the interval that spans 8 notes.

An octave is from one letter name to the **same** letter name, up or down.

1. Write the note that is one octave above the following notes. The first one is done for you.

2. Write the note that is one octave below the following notes.

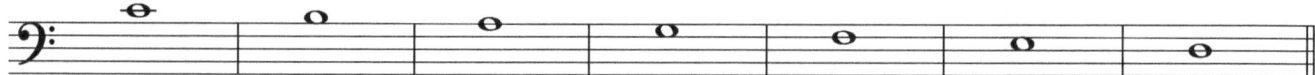

Transposition involves moving a group of notes up or down. In this level we are going to transpose by writing melodies up and down one octave in the same clef.

Figure 1.3 shows a short melody transposed up one octave in the the treble clef. The key and rhythm remain the same, but the stem direction changes.

Figure 1.3

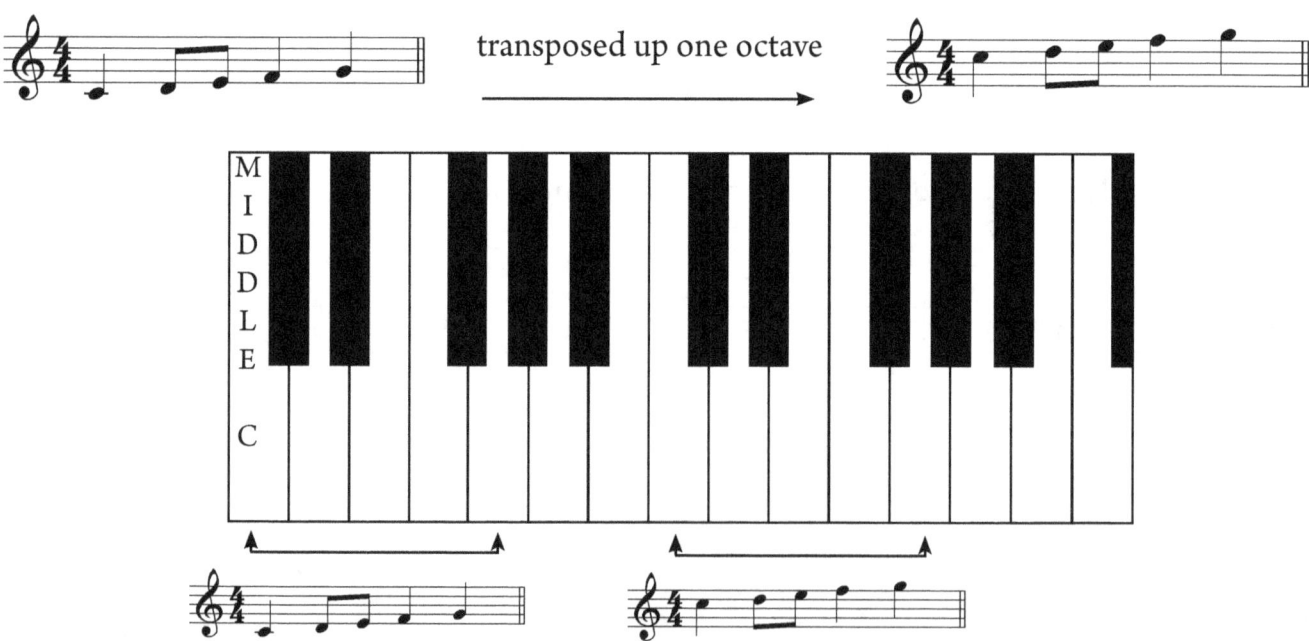

Notation

Figure 1.4 contains a melody in G major transposed down one octave in the bass clef. The key signature, time signature, and rhythm remain the same. Every note is moved down one octave and the normal rules of stem direction are followed.

Figure 1.4

original melody   transposed down one octave in the same clef

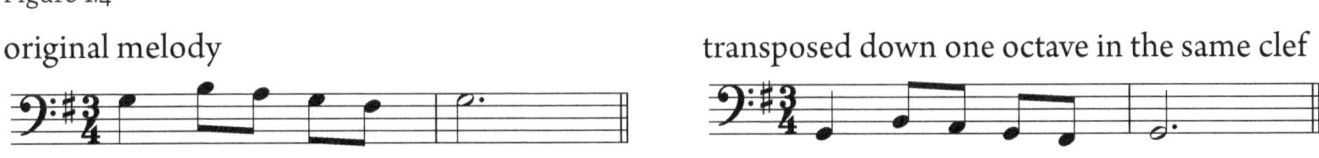

1. Transpose the following melody up one octave in the treble clef.

2. Transpose the following melody down one octave in the bass clef.

3. Transpose the following melody up one octave in the bass clef.

2
Rhythm and Meter

The Sixteenth Note

There are 16 sixteenth notes in a whole note. This makes the sixteenth note ¼ of a beat. One quarter note is equal to 4 sixteenth notes. A single sixteenth note has two flags attached to the stem. These flags are always placed on the right of the stem. When sixteenth notes are grouped together their stems are joined by two beams. Figure 2.1 show single sixteenth notes with flags and groups of sixteenth notes joined by beams.

Figure 2.1

Counting Sixteenth Notes

When we write sixteenth notes the beat is split up into four parts. We can assign each part a word or name. When you count say: 1 ee and ah (1 e + a). This divides the beat into four equal sections. Figure 2.2 shows a measure of sixteenth notes with counting.

Figure 2.2

Chart of Relative Note Values

Each note in the following chart has twice the value of the next one below it.

1 Whole Note	𝅝
equals	
2 Half Notes	𝅗𝅥 𝅗𝅥
equal	
4 Quarter Notes	♩ ♩ ♩ ♩
equal	
8 Eighth Notes	♫♫ ♫♫
equal	
16 Sixteenth Notes	♬♬♬♬

Rest Review

These are the rests studied in previous levels. When writing rests be sure to place them in the correct place on the staff. The placement is the same for the treble and bass staff.

Figure 2.3

Whole   Half   Quarter   Eighth

The Sixteenth Rest

A sixteenth rest looks like eighth rest with an extra flag on it. The flags are placed in the second and third space of the staff. This rest has the same value as a sixteenth note, ¼ of a beat

Figure 2.4

1. Circle the note or rest with the shortest duration.

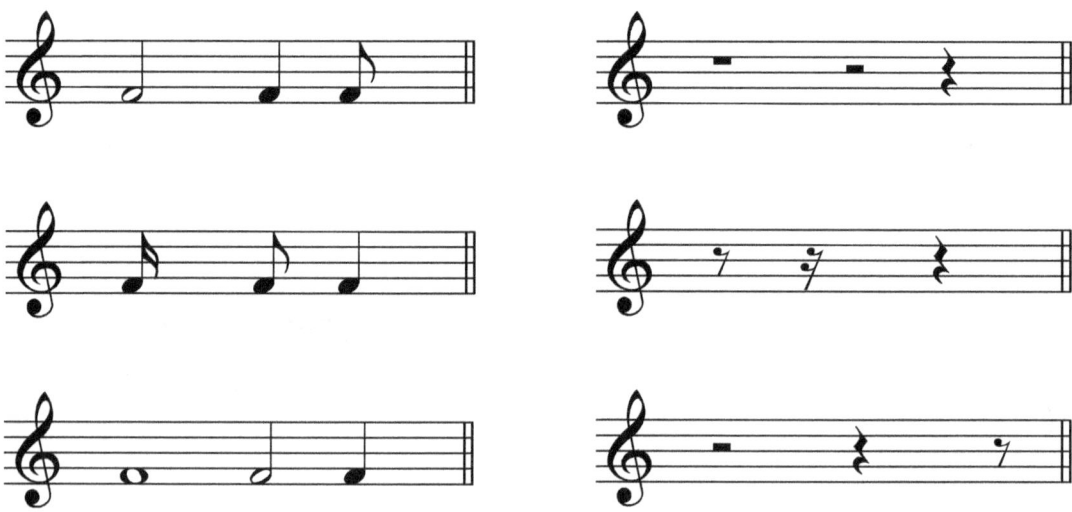

2. Circle the note or rest with the longest duration.

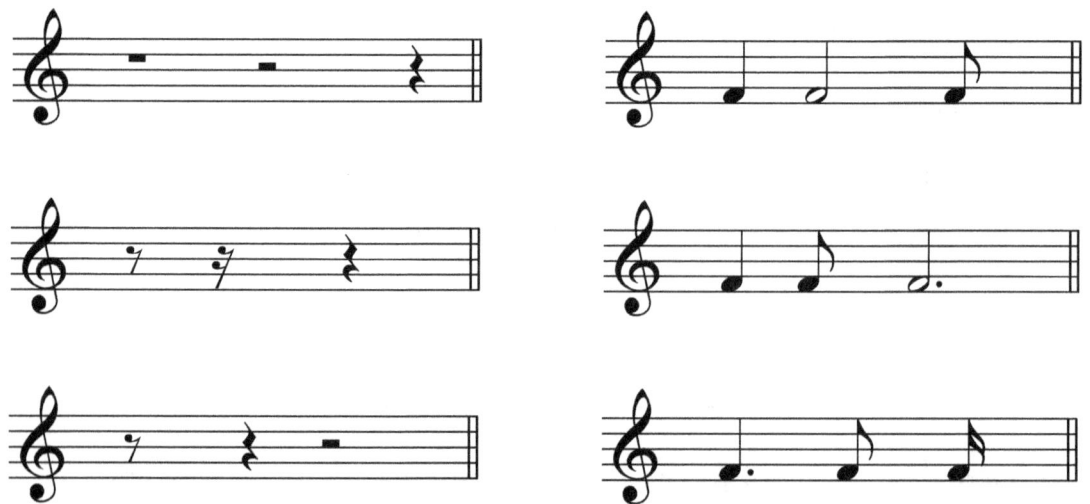

Joining Notes

Notes with flags are usually grouped together with beams to show one beat. Figure 2.5 shows how notes are grouped with beams to indicate one complete beat.

Figure 2.5

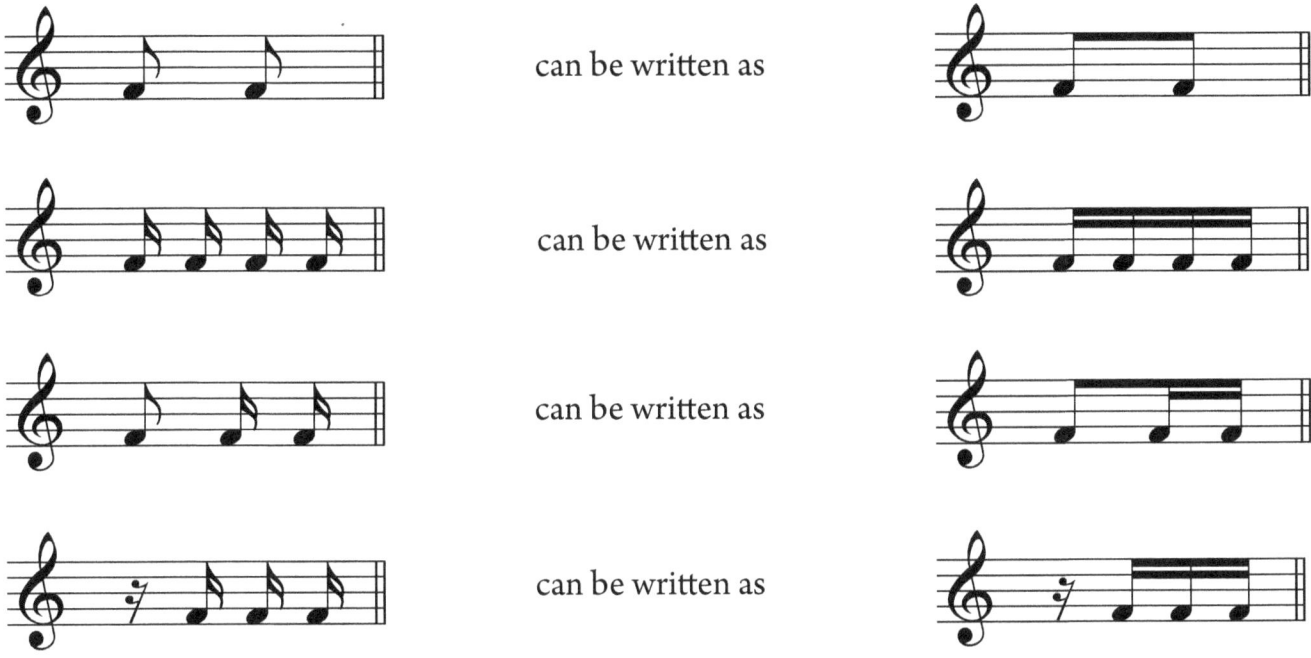

1. Rewrite the following joining the notes with beams wherever possible.

2. Answer the following questions.

   a) A whole note equals how many half notes? _____

   b) A half note equals how many quarter notes? _____

   c) A quarter note equals how many eighth notes? _____

   d) A quarter note equals how many sixteenth notes? _____

   e) An eighth note equals how many sixteenth notes? _____

3. Write **one** note which is equal to the following groups of notes.

4. Add time signatures at the beginning of each line.

5. Add **one** rest to complete each measure.

Dotted Eighth Notes

A dot after a note increases its value by half. Figure 2.8 contains a dotted half worth 3 beats and a dotted quarter worth 1 ½ beats.

Figure 2.8

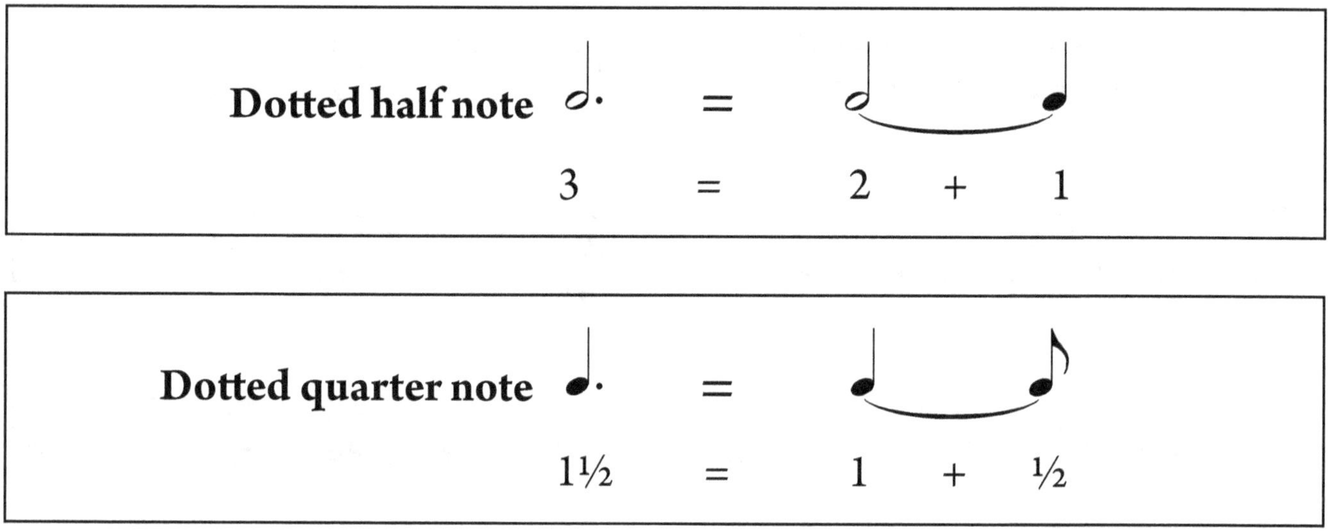

Dotted half note 𝅗𝅥.	=	𝅗𝅥 ⌣ 𝅘𝅥
3	=	2 + 1

Dotted quarter note 𝅘𝅥.	=	𝅘𝅥 ⌣ 𝅘𝅥𝅮
1½	=	1 + ½

Figure 2.9 contains a dotted eighth note. An eighth note is worth ½ of a beat. The dot is equal to a sixteenth note. A sixteenth note is worth ¼ of a beat. The dotted eighth is equal to ¾ of a beat.

Figure 2.9

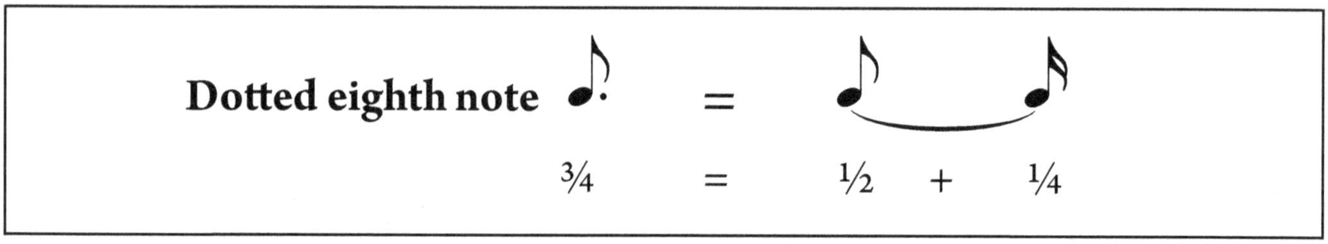

Dotted eighth note 𝅘𝅥𝅮.	=	𝅘𝅥𝅮 ⌣ 𝅘𝅥𝅯
¾	=	½ + ¼

Think of a dotted eighth note like a pie. The whole pie is 1 beat. An eighth note is ½ of the pie and a sixteenth note is ¼ of the pie. A dotted eighth (½ + ¼) is ¾ of the pie, or ¾ of a beat.

Figure 2.10

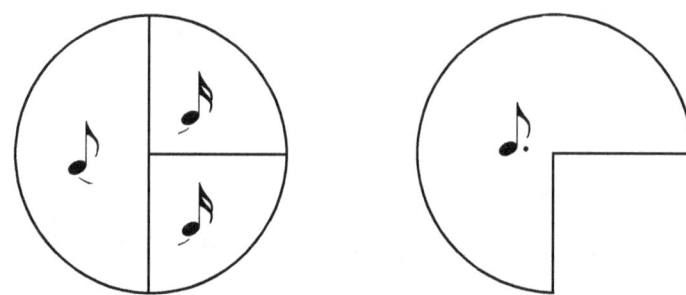

The dotted eighth note is often seen in combination with a sixteenth note as shown in Figure 2.11. The dotted eighth is connected by a beam to a sixteenth note. This creates one complete beat and is a common rhythmic figure.

Figure 2.11

1. Draw a line connecting each group of notes with its corresponding note value.

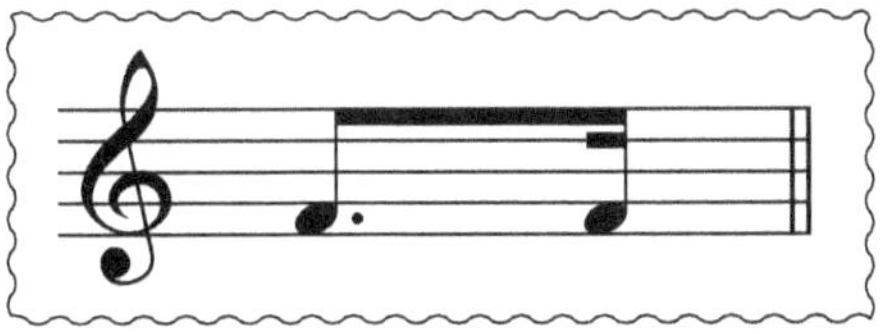

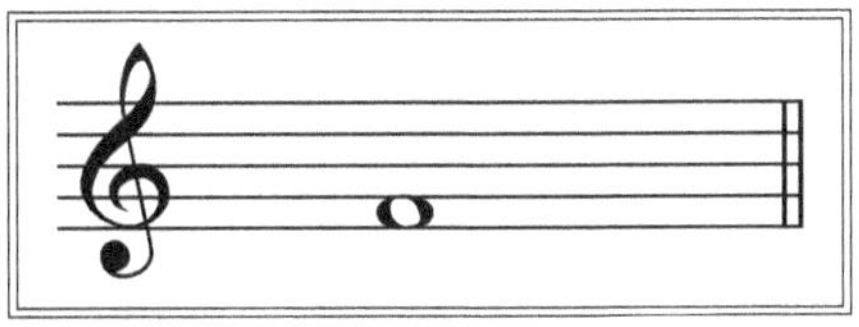

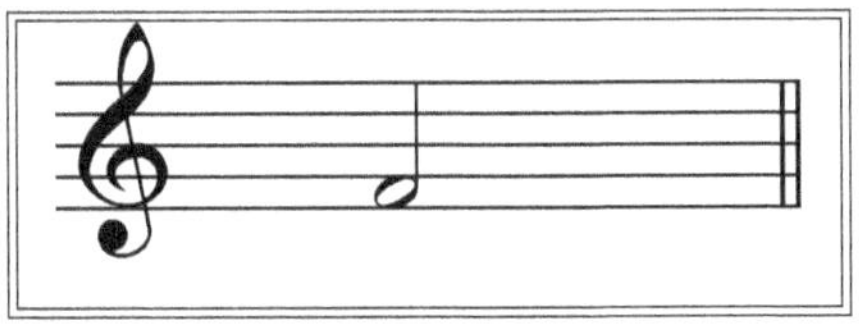

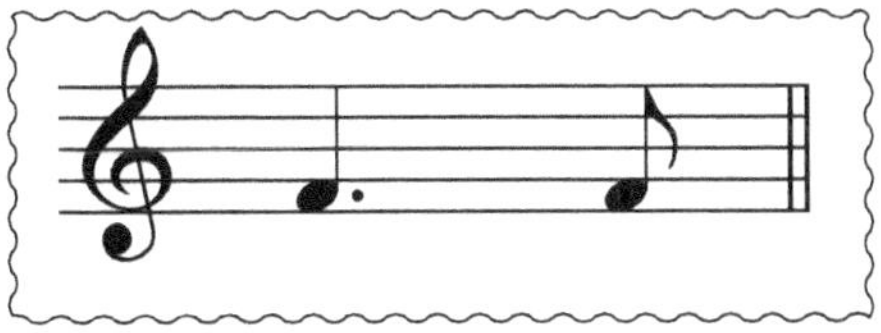

2. Add the missing bar lines to the following musical examples.

The Upbeat or Anacrusis

The first beat of a measure is the strongest and is called the **downbeat**. Some pieces begin on an unaccented or less strong beat. This is called an **upbeat, pickup,** or **anacrusis**.

When a melody begins on an upbeat, both the first and last measure will be incomplete. Figure 2.12 contains a melody that begins on an upbeat. It begins on beat 3, a weak beat. The first note of this melody is a quarter note upbeat. The first and last measures of this melody are incomplete. The third beat which is missing from the last measure is equal to the upbeat in the first measure. These two incomplete measures add up to one complete measure. No rests are needed with incomplete measures.

Figure 2.12

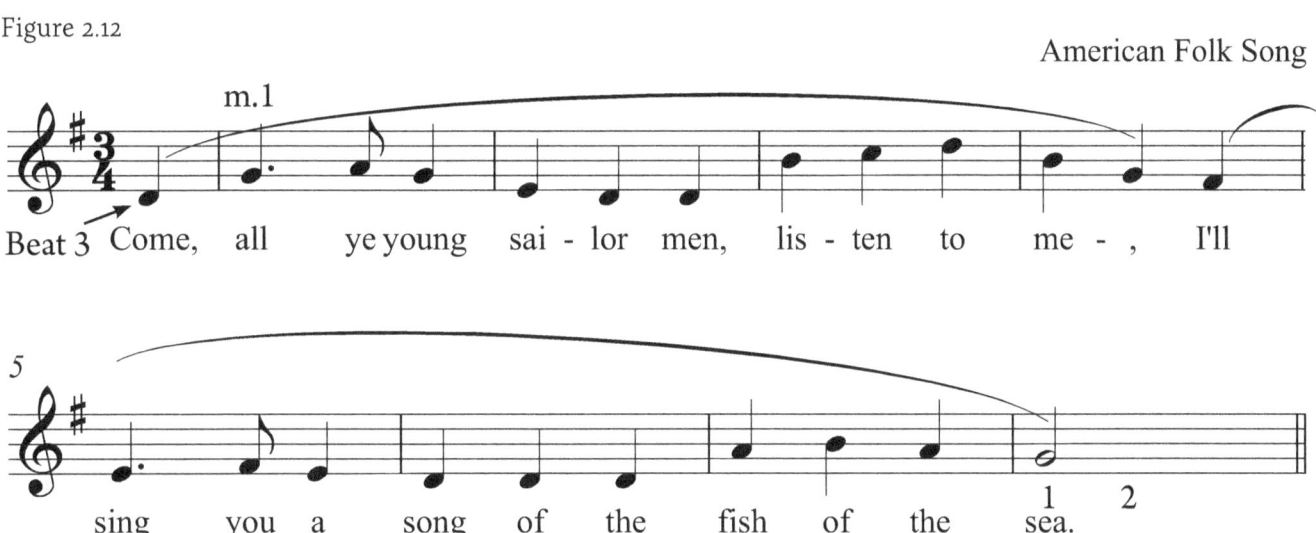

Review - The Phrase

Most traditional melodies move in four measure sections called **phrases**. A phrase is a musical sentence. Like the sentence in a story, a phrase represents one musical idea. Phrases are often indicated by a long curved line called a **phrase mark**. A phrase mark looks like a large slur. This line indicates the beginning and end of the phrase. Figure 2.12 has phrase marks above the melody. This melody consists of two four measures phrases.

In Figure 2.12 each 4 measure phrase begins with an upbeat. When a piece begins with an upbeat, often each of the following phrases will also begin with an upbeat. This is a feature which unifies the music.

Measure numbers are an important feature in music. They help us when learning, analyzing, or rehearsing. In a piece that begins with an incomplete measure, the incomplete measure is not numbered. The first measure (m.1), is the bar after the anacrusis. This measure contains the first strong beat in the piece and is considered m.1. See Figure 2.12.

1. Name the key of the following melodies. Find and circle the upbeats (anacrusis) in each one. Mark the phrases with a slur.

Allegretto

key:

Allegro

key:

Rhythm and Meter

Rests in Simple Time

The time signatures we have studied, 2/4, 3/4, and 4/4, are considered *simple time* signatures. In simple time each beat can be divided evenly into 2, or 4.

When writing rests in simple time, any incomplete beats must be completed first. Figure 2.13 illustrates how to complete single quarter note beats in simple time.

Figure 2.13 a) and b): An eighth note requires an eighth rest to complete the quarter note beat.
Figure 2.13 c): Each part of the beat is completed before beginning the next part.
Figure 2.13 d): The beat is completed in order, with the 16th note and rest occuring together.
Figure 2.13 e): A dotted eighth requires a 16th rest to complete the beat.

Figure 2.13

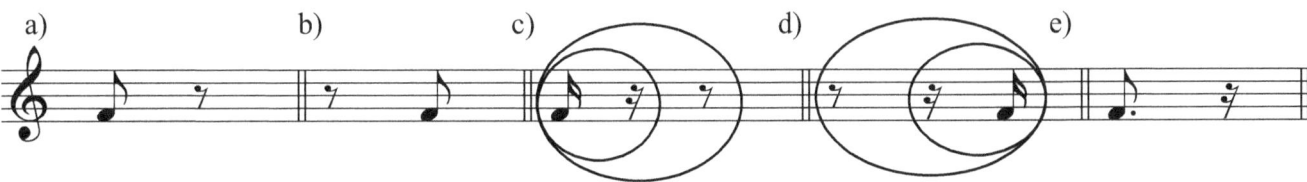

There are specific rules for adding rests to a measure in simple time. It is important to show each beat as clearly as possible. Each beat or each part of the beat must be completed before beginning the next beat. In Figure 2.14 measure 2, each eighth note beat is completed with an eighth note rest. In measures 3 and 4, the sixteenth note has a sixteenth rest to complete part of the beat and then an eighth rest to complete the remainder of the beat.

Figure 2.14

In 3/4 time each beat or part of the beat should be completed first. Join beats 1 and 2, a strong and weak beat, into one rest. **Do not join beats 2 and 3, two weak beats, into one rest.** Never join two weak beats into one rest.

Figure 2.15

We never use rests larger than one beat unless it is in the first half or last half of a measure in 4/4 time. Never join beats 2 and 3, a weak beat and a medium beat, into one rest. As in all simple time signatures, finish any incomplete beats first.

Figure 2.16

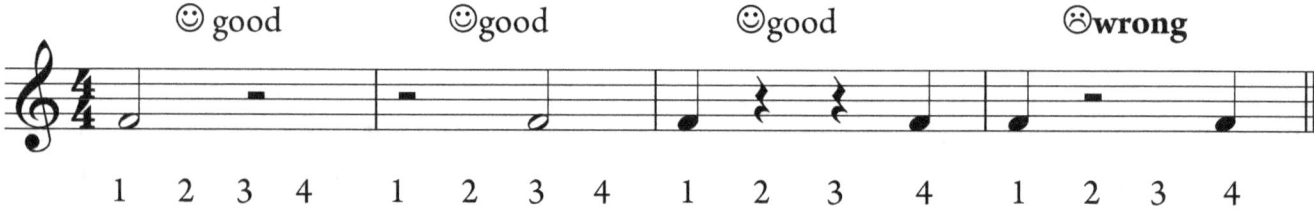

In 2/4, 3/4, and 4/4 time the whole rest is used to show one complete measure of silence. Always use a whole rest to indicate a whole measure of silence in these time signatures.

Figure 2.17

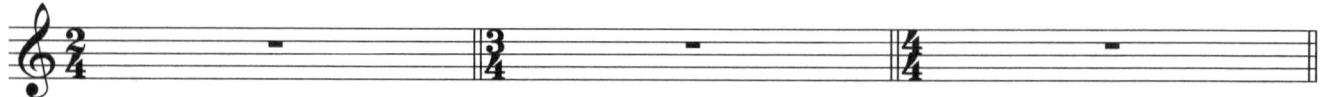

We have not studied dotted rests since they are not used in simple time. Dotted notes are fine, but never use dotted rests in 2/4, 3/4, or 4/4 time. Dotted rests will be covered later.

1. Complete each quarter note beat by adding rests under the brackets.

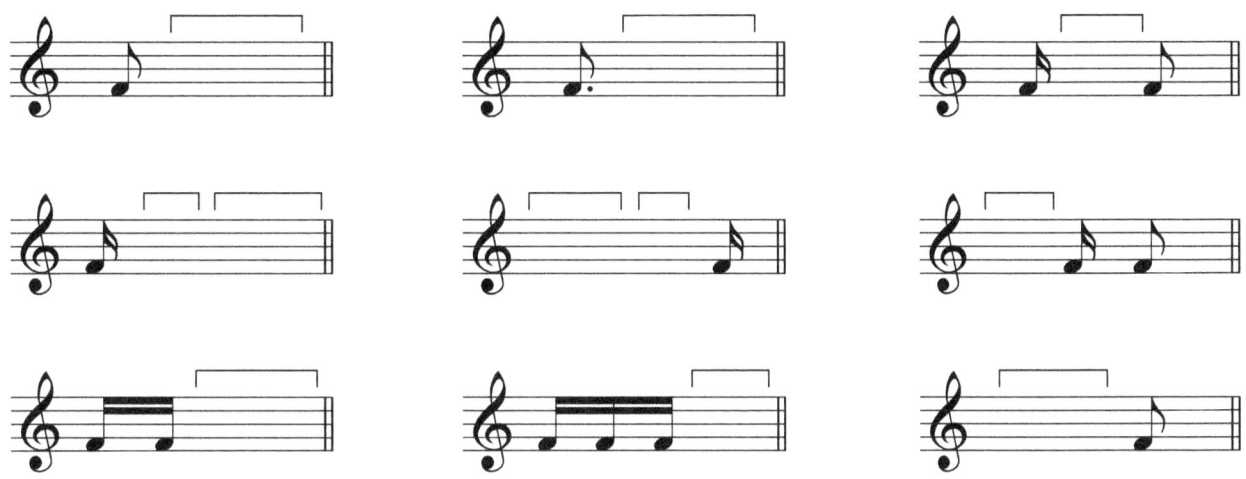

2. Mark each measure in the following examples as ☑ if the rests are correct, or ☒ if the rests are incorrect.

3. Add one rest under each bracket to complete the following measures.

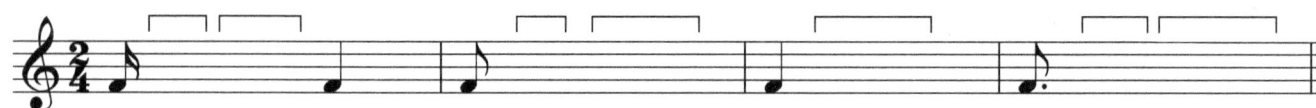

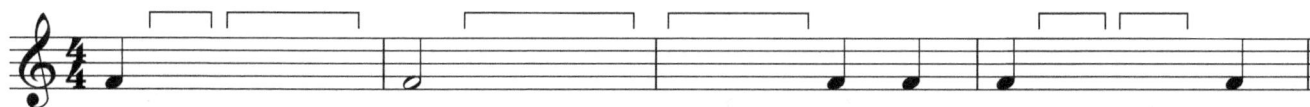

4. Add rests under the brackets to complete each measure. There may be more than one rest under each bracket.

3
Major Scales

Key Signatures

A key signature contains the sharps and flats in a piece of music and tells a performer on what scale the piece is based. The key signature is placed at the beginning of a piece of music between the clef and time signature. The order of sharps and flats in a key signature is always the same. You will never have mixed sharps and flats. It will be all sharps, all flats, or no accidentals at all. Key signatures of major scales are determined by the order of whole steps and half steps in the scale.

Figure 3.1 contains the D major scale. There are two sharps in this scale (F♯ and C♯) that result from following the order of whole and half steps required for a major scale (W W H W W W H).

Figure 3.1

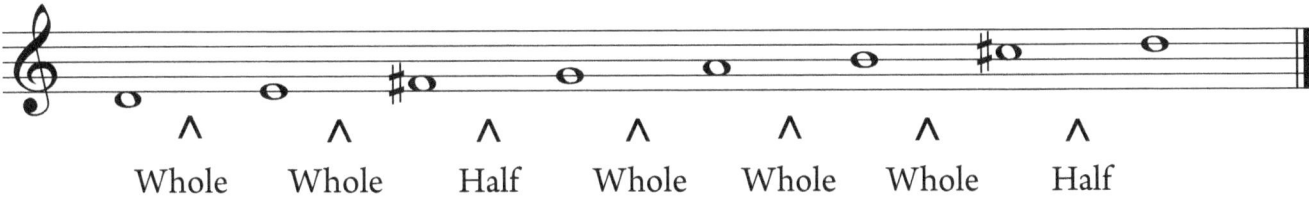

Figure 3.2 shows that if you build a major scale on B♭ using the same order of whole and half steps you get a scale with two flats (B♭ and E♭).

Figure 3.2

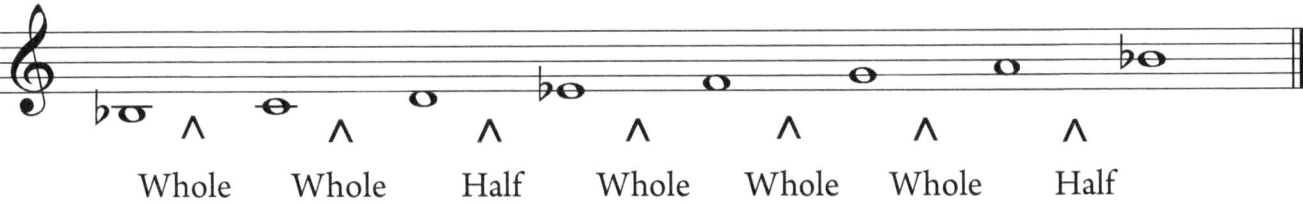

Here are the key signatures on the grand staff for keys up to two sharps and flats.

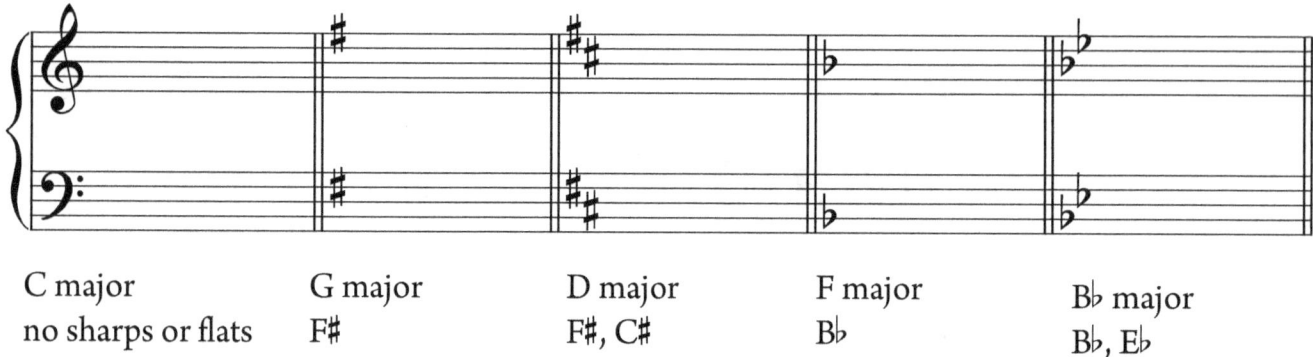

C major   G major   D major   F major   B♭ major
no sharps or flats   F♯   F♯, C♯   B♭   B♭, E♭

1. Write the following key signatures on the grand staff.

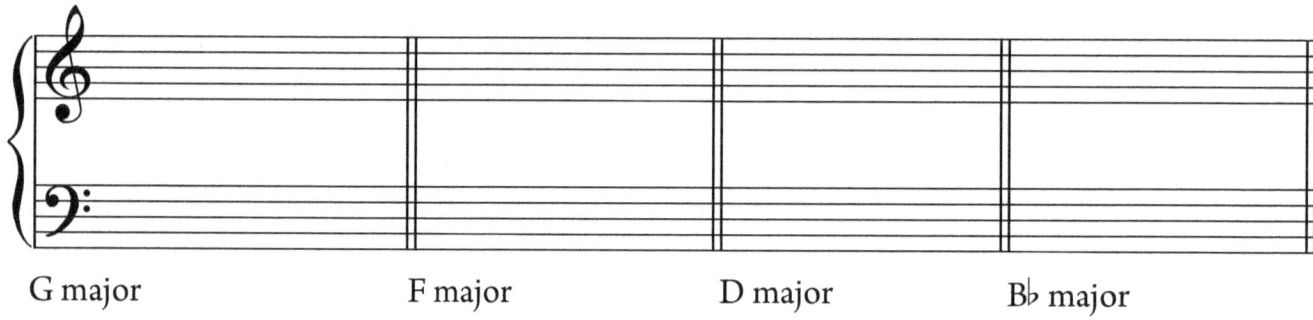

G major   F major   D major   B♭ major

Each scale can be labelled with a scale degree ($\hat{1}$, $\hat{2}$, $\hat{3}$, etc.). There are also technical names for the scale degrees. $\hat{1}$ is the tonic, $\hat{4}$ is the subdominant and $\hat{5}$ is the dominant. Scale degree $\hat{7}$ is known as the leading tone. This is because it is a half step away from, and leads to the tonic. Play a major scale and stop on the leading tone. Listen to the pull the leading tone has to the tonic note.

Figure 3.3

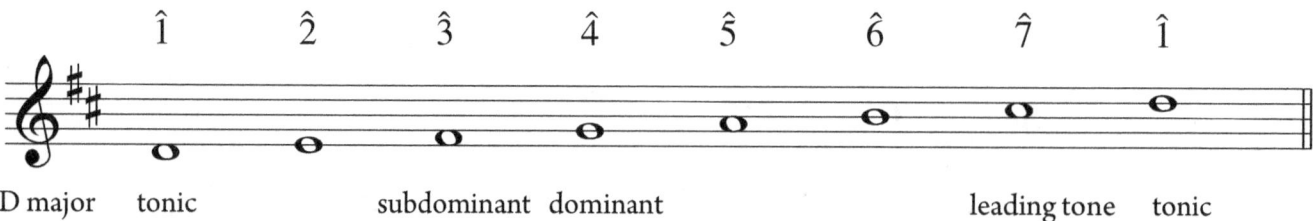

D major   tonic   subdominant dominant   leading tone tonic

Major Scales

1. Write the following scales ascending and descending using a key signature for each. Label the leading tone (LT).

D major in half notes

F major in quarter notes

G major in single sixteenth notes

C major in whole notes

B♭ major in dotted half notes

Major Scales

2. Add clefs and key signatures to complete the following major scales. Mark the half steps with a slur and label the tonic (T), dominant (D), and leading tones (LT).

B♭ major

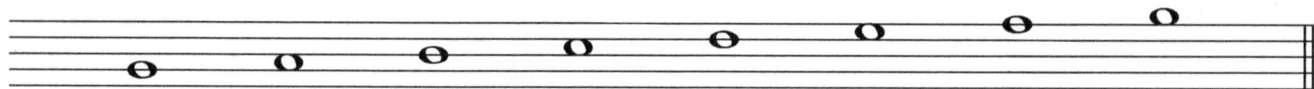

D major

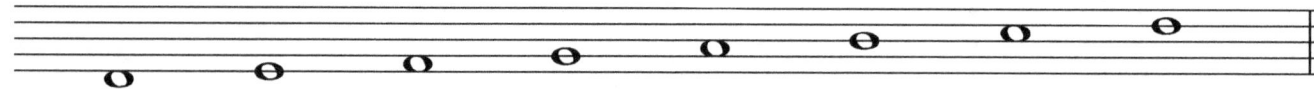

F major

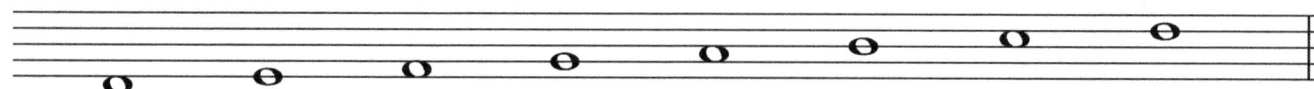

G major

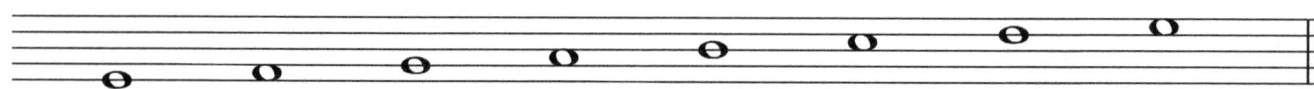

C major

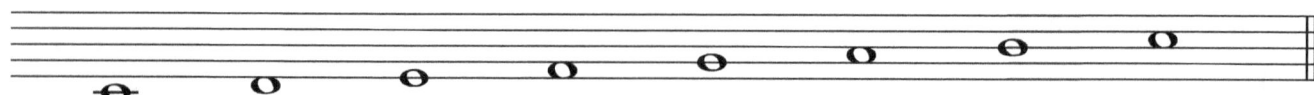

Major Scales

3. Identify the following major key signatures.

Key: _____ _____ _____ _____ _____

4. Write the following scales ascending and descending in whole notes using accidentals instead of a key signature.

The major scale with 2 flats

key:

The major scale with 1 sharp

key:

The major scale with 1 flat

key:

The major scale with 2 sharps

key:

Major Scales

5. Answer the following questions.

   a. Name the leading tone of the F major scale: _____

   b. Name the dominant of the G major scale: _____

   c. Name the subdominant of the B♭ major scale: _____

   d. Name the tonic of the D major scale: _____

   e. Name the leading tone of the C major scale: _____

6. Write the following scales ascending and descending in half notes using a key signature for each.

The major scale with C♯ as the leading tone

The major scale with C as the dominant

The major scale with C as the subdominant

Major Scales

4
History 1

Music Terms

Terms Relating to Style

Musical terms relating to *style* tell us how something is to be performed. Composers may ask you to play sweetly, or majestically, or gracefully. There are Italian terms that are universally used in music to indicate these and many other styles. Here are a few.

cantabile	in a singing style
dolce	sweet
grazioso	graceful
maestoso	majestic
marcato, marc.	marked or stressed

Johann Sebastian Bach (1685 - 1750) Baroque Era

Johann Sebastian Bach was born in Eisenach, Germany where his father, a musician, taught him to play violin and harpsichord. Many of Bach's relatives were also musicians. His older brother, Johann Christoph Bach taught him to play the organ.

In 1707, Bach married his cousin Maria Barbara Bach. They had seven children. Maria died, and Bach married Anna Magdalena Wilcke in 1721. They had 13 more children. In total, Bach had 20 children. Some of Bach's sons became well-known composers. Carl Phillip Emmanuel Bach and Johann Christian Bach are two of them.

One of Bach's first serious jobs was working for a duke. After that, he was hired to compose for a prince. His final job was the director of music at St. Thomas Church and School in Leipzig, Germany. Here he was cantor (music teacher), organist, and music composer. He was very busy teaching, conducting, performing, and writing music. While in Leipzig he conducted a small group of local musicians who sometimes played at coffee houses.

Bach wrote a lot of music. His works fill many large volumes and contain, choral music, concertos, orchestra and chamber music and organ and keyboard music. Some of Bachs most famous compositions are the Brandenburg Concertos and The Well Tempered Clavier, written as teaching pieces for his students. He also wrote many great works for organ including the famous Toccata and Fugue in D minor.

Bach is considered one of the greatest musicians and composers that ever lived. However, during his life, he was hardly known. About 100 years after his death another composer named Felix Mendelssohn brought attention to his music, and the world finally realized Bach's greatness.

Bach composed during the Baroque era, which was between the years 1600 and 1750. Baroque music has tuneful melodies and can be very dramatic. The melodies are often very elaborate and decorated with trills and ornaments. Bach died in 1750.

Review 1

1. In the empty measures write the enhamonic equivalent of the previous notes. Name each note.

2. Connect each group of four eighth notes with stems and beams.

3. Add stems and flags for the following single sixteenth notes.

4. Add the correct time signature at the beginning of each line.

5. Add one rest to complete each measure.

6. Write the following major key signatures on the grand staff.

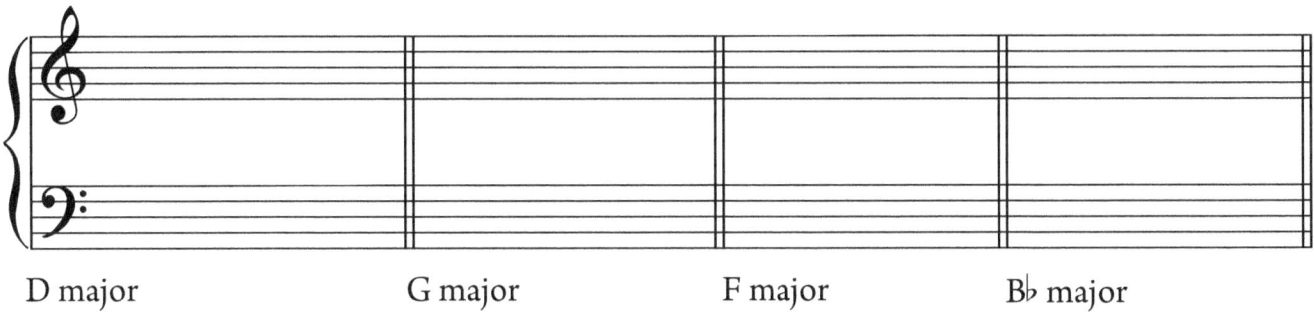

D major   G major   F major   B♭ major

7. Write the following scales ascending and descending using a key signature for each. Label the tonic, (T), Subdominant (SD), dominant (D), and leading note (LN).

B♭ major in whole notes

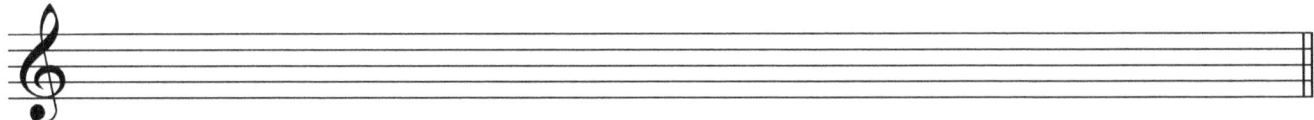

D major in quarter notes

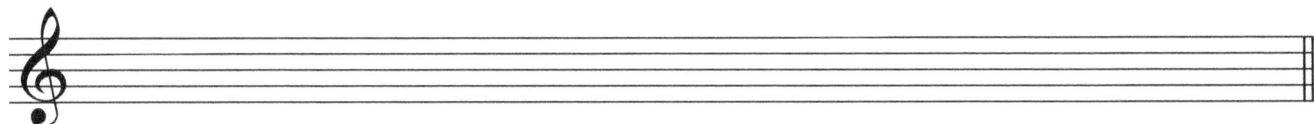

G major in single eighth notes

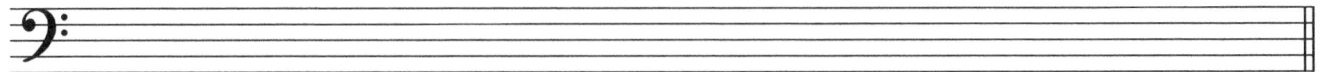

8. Name the key of the following melody and transpose it down one octave in the treble clef.

key:

9. Answer the following questions.

a) In what musical era did J.S. Bach live? _____

b) What are his first two names? _____ _____ Bach.

c) In what country was he born? _____

d) What instruments did his father teach him to play? _____

e) How many children did he have? _____

f) Name two of his sons. _____ _____

g) Check all the jobs Bach did.

☐ organist ☐ cantor ☐ pianist ☐ composer ☐ farmer ☐ teacher

h) Who helped to revive his music 100 years after his death? _____

i) What year does the Baroque era end? _____

10. Match the music term with its meaning.

_____ *cantabile*   a) majestic

_____ *dolce*   b) marked or stressed

_____ *grazioso*   c) sweet

_____ *maestoso*   d) in a singing style

_____ *marcato, marc.*   e) graceful

5

Minor Scales

Minor Scale Review

The ***natural minor scale*** was covered in Level 2. If you play a major scale from the 6th note to the 6th note you get a natural minor scale. The C major scale played from A to A, produces the A natural minor scale (Figure 5.1). All of the notes in A natural minor come from the C major scale. A minor is the ***relative minor*** of C major. A minor and C major are related by key signature. They each have the same number of flats or sharps. C major's relative minor is A minor, and A minor's relative major is C major. Both keys have no sharps or flats in their key signature.

The natural minor scale made up of a specific pattern of whole and half steps. It is constructed using the pattern WHWWHWW. The half steps occur between $\hat{2}$ and $\hat{3}$ and $\hat{5}$ and $\hat{6}$. Figure 5.1 contains the A natural minor scale using this interval pattern. Using this pattern you can construct a natural minor scale on any note.

Figure 5.1

C major

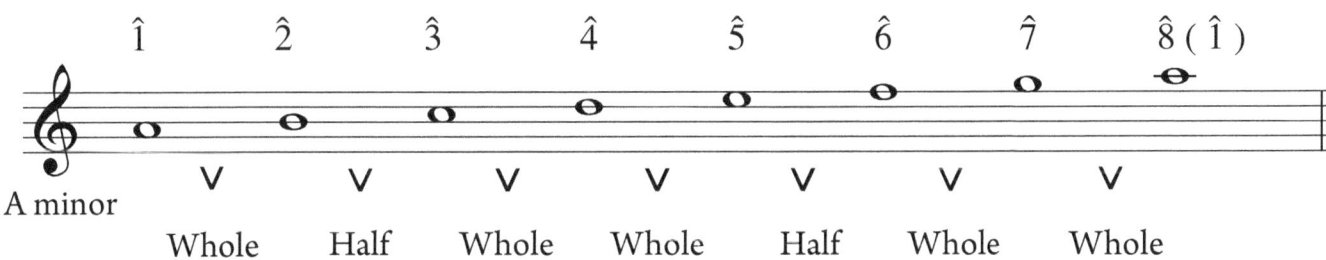

A minor

Minor Scales

Relative Minor Keys

Every major key has a relative minor. They are related because they share the same key signature. C major and A minor have no sharps or flats. C major is the relative major of A minor and vice versa.

To determine a minor key signature:

1. Name the major key.

2. Count up six notes (or down three) to get the relative minor key.

The 6th note of the D major scale is B. B minor has the same key signature as D major, two sharps, F# and C#. Every key signature reflects two keys, one major and one minor.

Figure 5.2

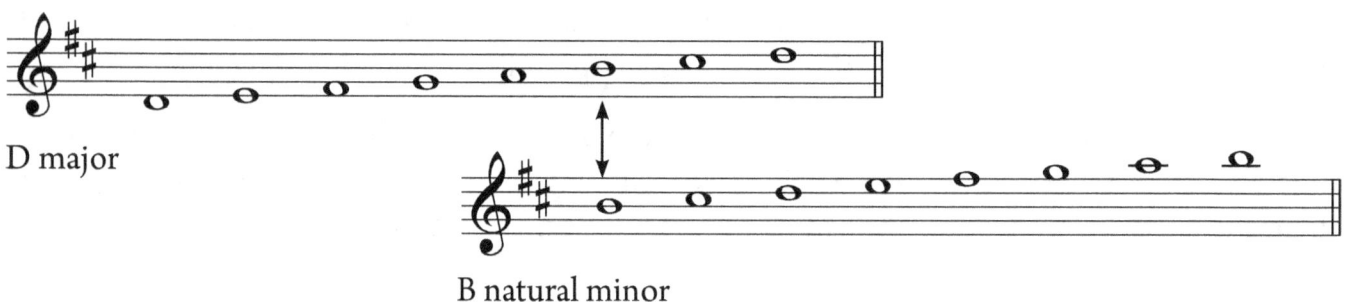

D major

B natural minor

Figure 5.3 contains the relative major and minor keys up to two sharps and flats.

Figure 5.3

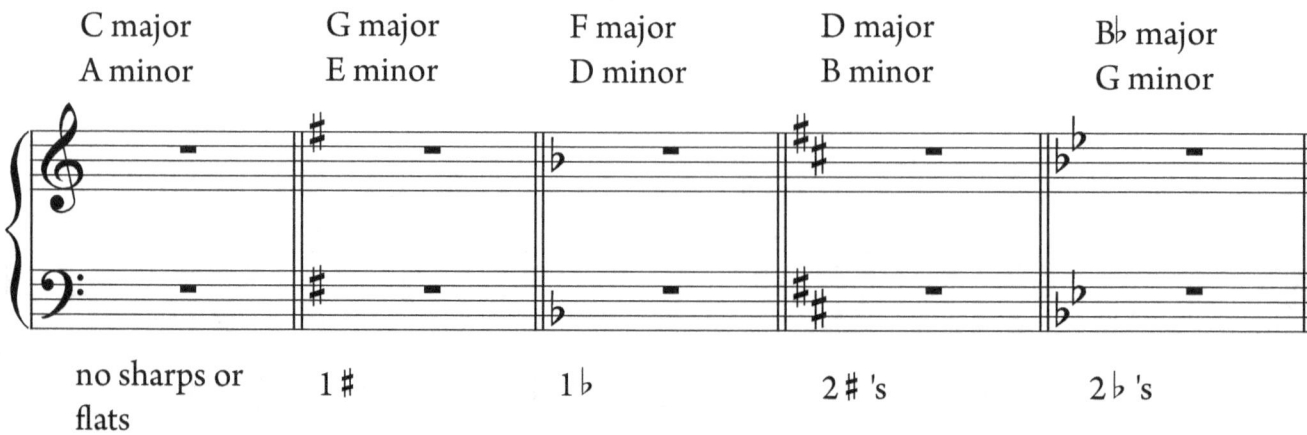

Minor Scales

1. Name the following relative major and minor keys for the following.

    D major _____   B minor _____

    E minor _____   A minor _____

    C major _____   G major _____

    F major _____   D minor _____

2. Write the following natural minor scales ascending and descending in whole notes using a key signature. Mark the half steps with a slur.

B natural minor

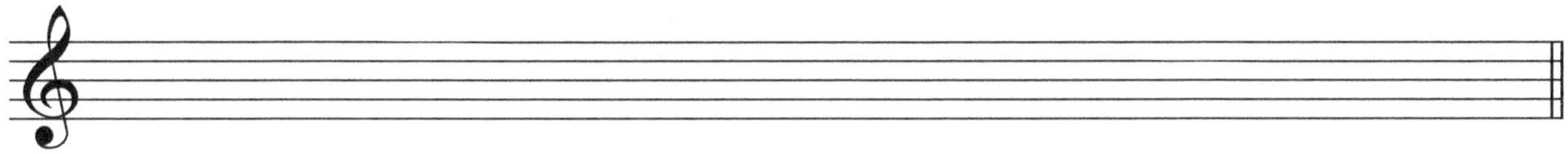

G natural minor

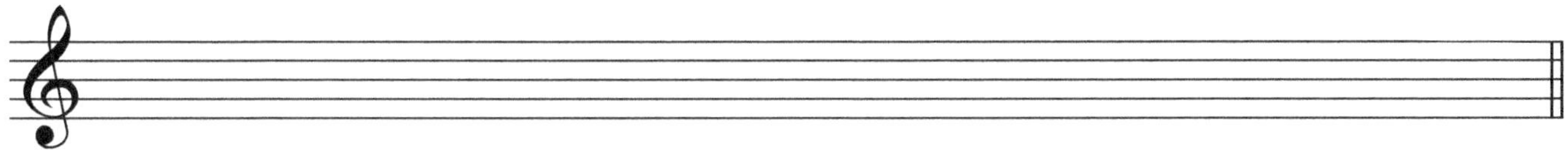

D natural minor

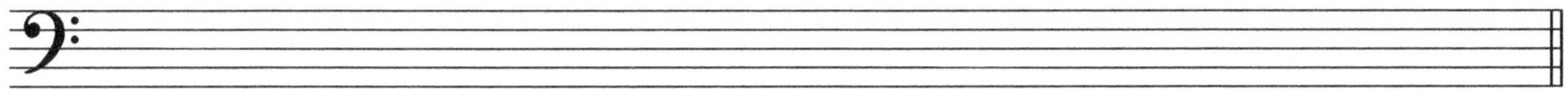

Minor Scales

The Harmonic Minor Scale

The **harmonic minor scale** is the most common minor scale. It is a slightly altered version of the natural minor scale. In the harmonic minor scale, $\hat{7}$ is raised one half step. The name harmonic comes from the way the scale is used. This version of the scale is required to get the music correct when writing chords. A half step is needed between $\hat{7}$ and $\hat{8}$ to create certain chord progressions in music. When $\hat{7}$ is a half step away from the tonic ($\hat{8}$), it is called the **leading tone** because it leads our ear to the tonic.

In the natural minor scale where $\hat{7}$ is not raised, and is a whole step away from the tonic, it is called the **subtonic**. When $\hat{7}$ is a whole step away it does not sound like it is leading to the tonic, so it is not called the leading tone. In minor keys we have two names for $\hat{7}$. When it is raised, it is called the **leading tone**. When it is not raised it is called the **subtonic**.

The harmonic minor uses the same key signature as the natural minor (the relative major), but there is an accidental for raised $\hat{7}$. Figure 5.4 contains the A natural minor scale and the A harmonic minor scale. A minor's relative major is C major so there are no sharps or flats in the key signature. The harmonic minor is simply the natural minor with $\hat{7}$ raised one half step. $\hat{7}$ is G and we use a sharp to raise it one half step to G♯. In the harmonic minor scale there are three half steps. They occur between $\hat{2}$ and $\hat{3}$, $\hat{5}$ and $\hat{6}$ and $\hat{7}$ and $\hat{8}$.

Figure 5.4

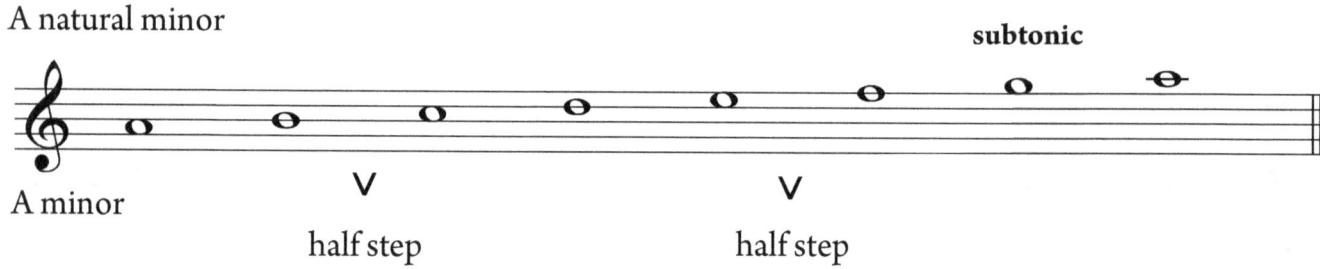

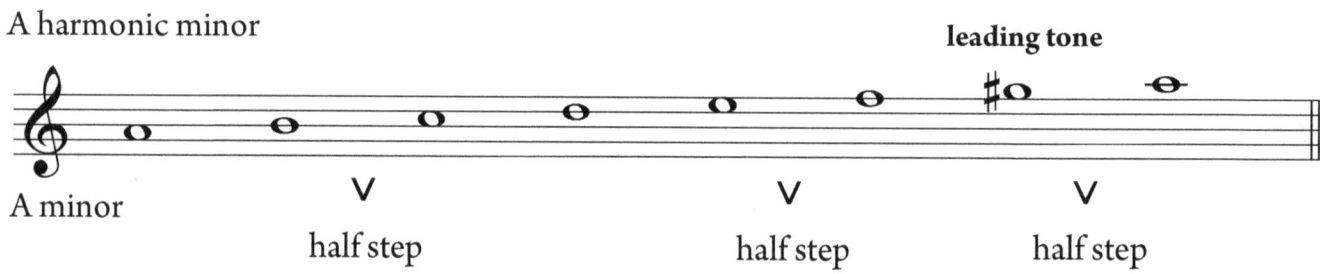

1. The following are natural minor scales. Name the key of each. Add accidentals making them harmonic minor scales. Mark the half steps with a slur.

key:

key:

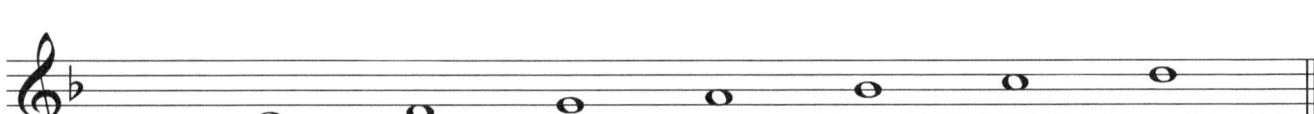

key:

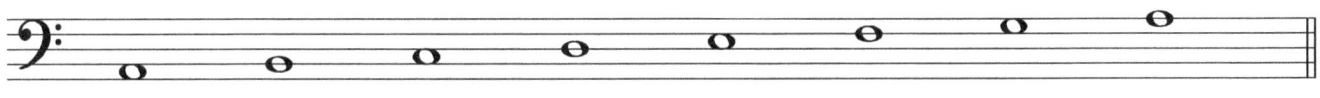

key:

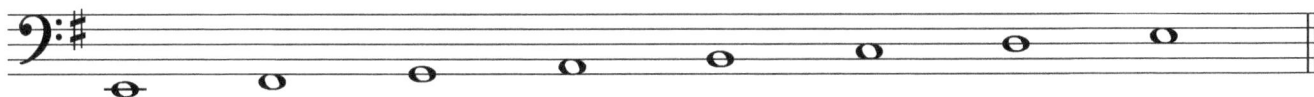

key:

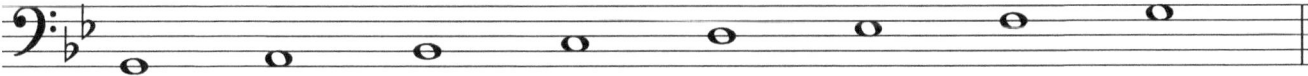

key:

2. Write the following scales ascending and descending in whole notes using a key signature. Label the leading tone (LT).

A harmonic minor

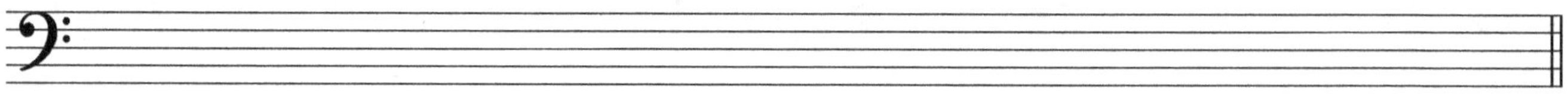

D harmonic minor

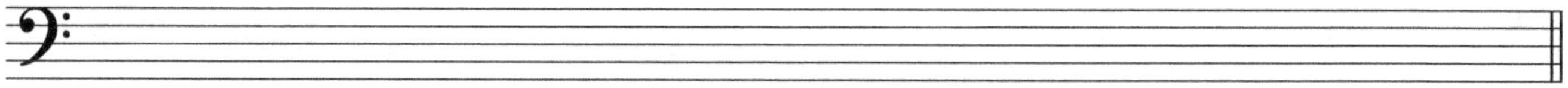

G harmonic minor

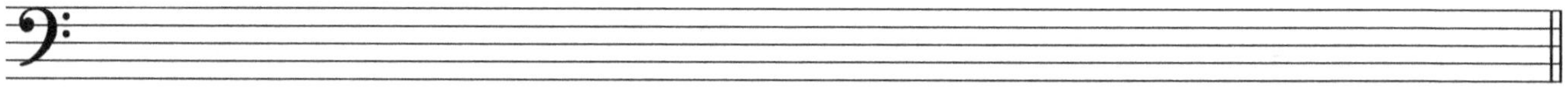

B harmonic minor

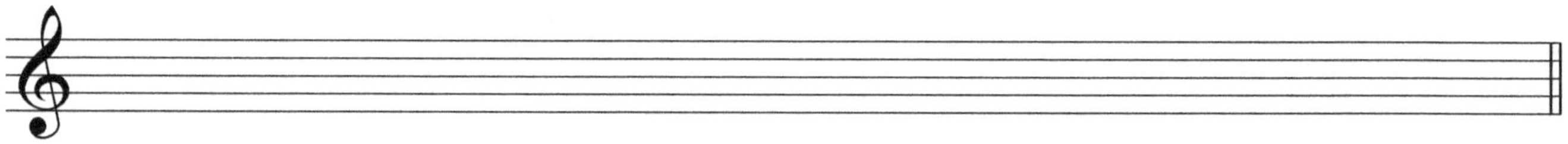

E harmonic minor

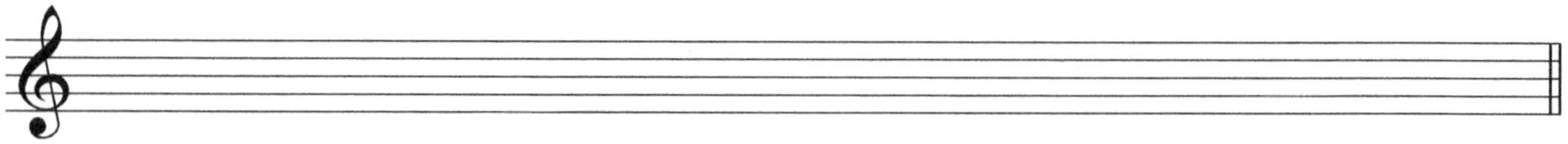

D harmonic minor

Minor Scales

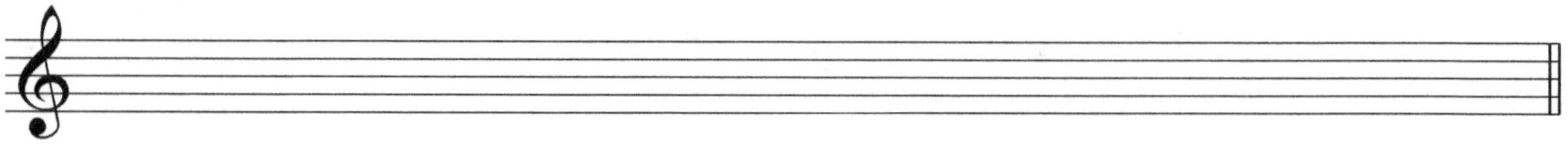

The Melodic Minor Scale

The *melodic minor scale* is based on the natural minor scale but contains altered notes. This scale is different ascending than it is descending.

On the way up, scale degrees $\hat{6}$ and $\hat{7}$ are raised one half step, and on the way down, they are lowered one half step. The whole point of this scale is to smooth out the space between $\hat{6}$ and $\hat{7}$. In the harmonic form of this scale, raised $\hat{7}$ is important when writing music and chords, but can sound strange when played by itself in the scale. When we raise and lower $\hat{6}$ and $\hat{7}$, the scale works better within a melody. Since this scale helps create smoother melodies, it is called the melodic minor scale.

Compare the A natural minor scale and the A melodic minor scale in Figure 5.4. In the melodic minor, $\hat{6}$ and $\hat{7}$ (F and G) are raised ascending and lowered descending. This scale contains both the leading tone (G♯) and the subtonic (G♮).

Figure 5.4

A natural minor

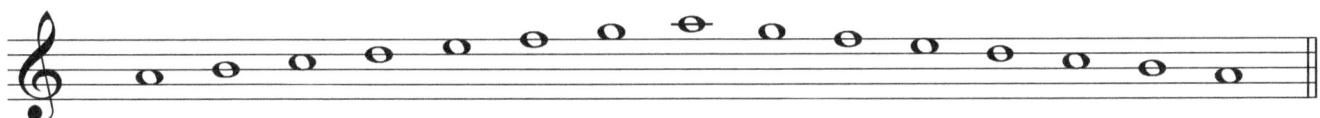

A melodic minor

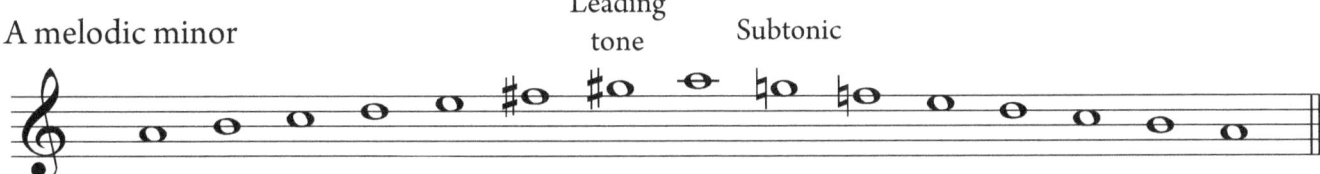

In a scale like G melodic minor you need to use a natural and a sharp to raise $\hat{6}$ and $\hat{7}$ ascending and a natural and flat to lower them descending (Figure 5.6).

Figure 5.6

1. The following are natural minor scales. Name the key of each. Add accidentals making them melodic minor scales. Mark the leading tone (LT) and subtonic (ST) in each.

key:

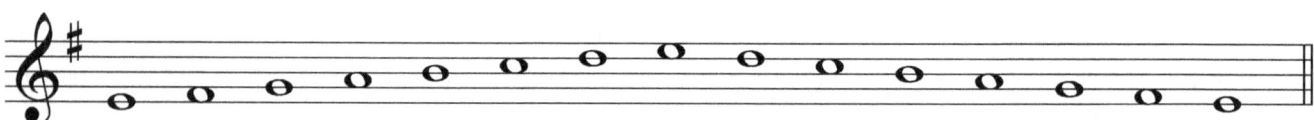

key:

key:

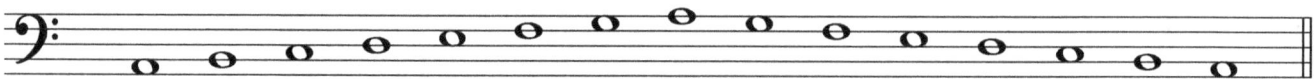

key:

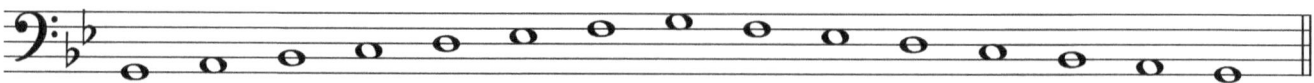

key:

Minor Scales

2. Write the following scales ascending and descending in whole notes using a key signature.

G melodic minor

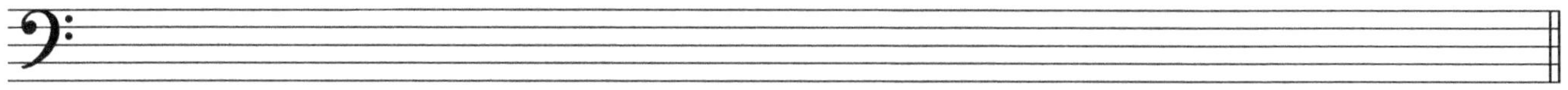

A melodic minor

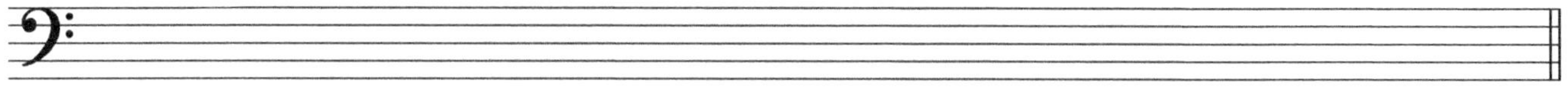

E melodic minor

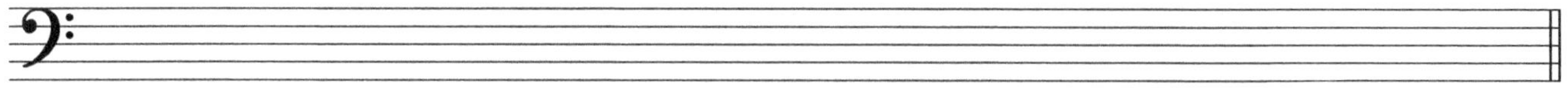

B melodic minor

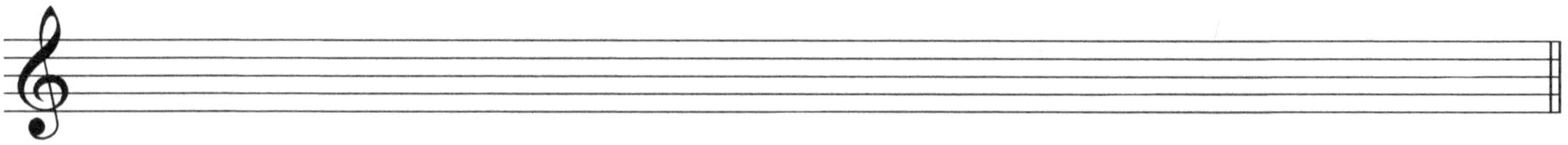

D melodic minor

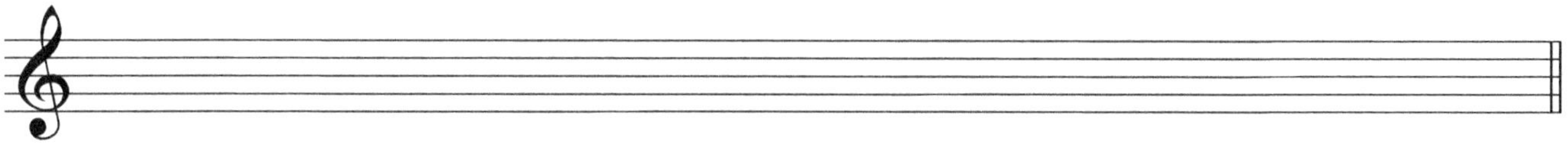

G melodic minor

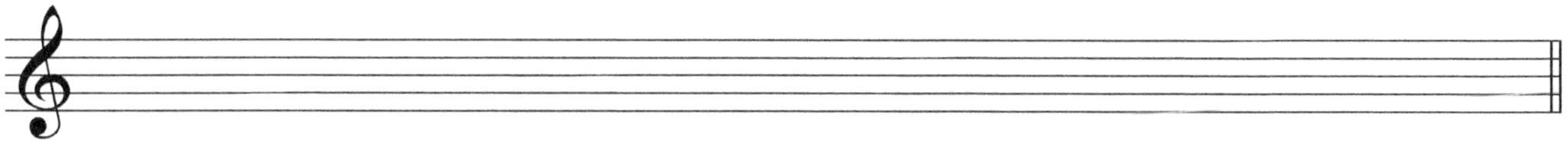

Minor Scales

3. Name the following minor scales.

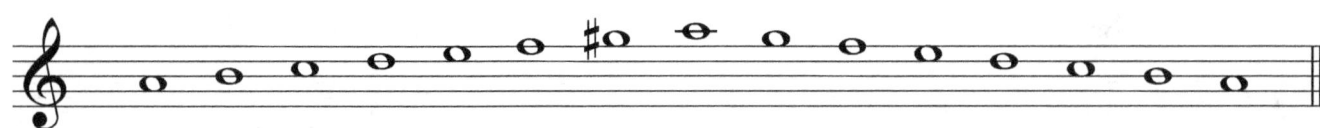

Scale: _____

Scale: _____

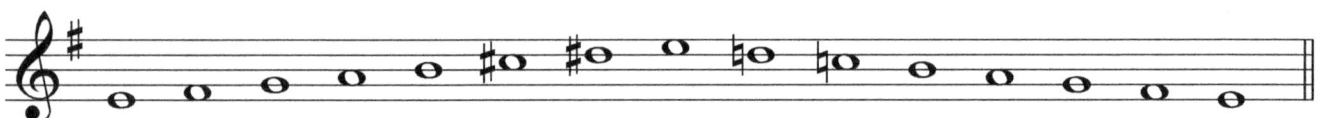

Scale: _____

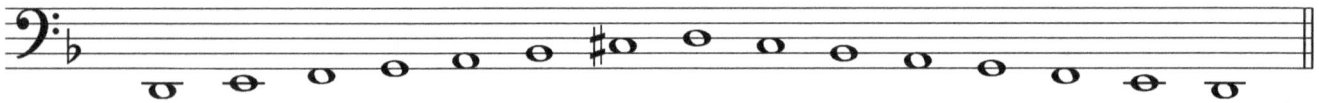

Scale: _____

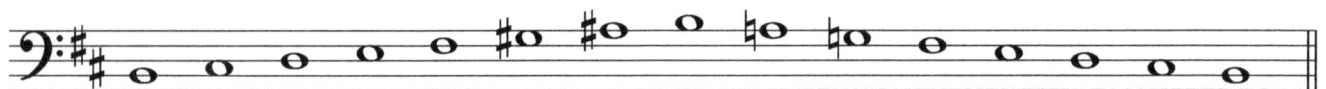

Scale: _____

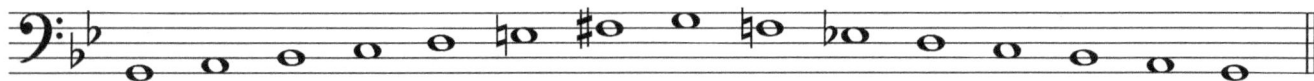

Scale: _____

4. Write the following scales ascending and descending in whole notes.

A melodic minor

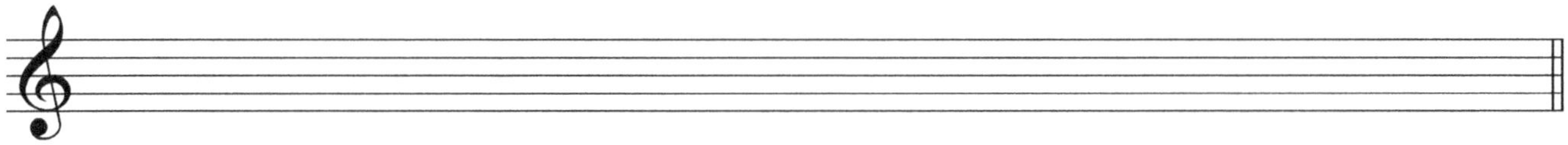

G harmonic minor

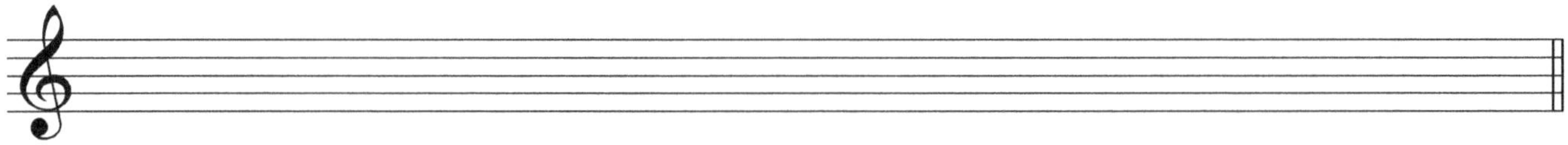

E melodic minor

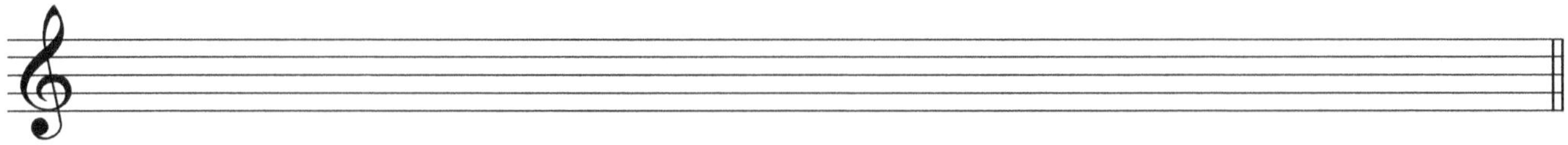

B harmonic minor

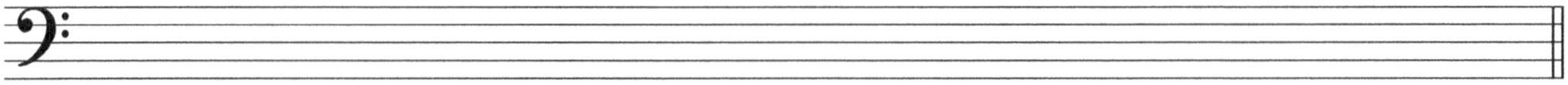

D natural minor

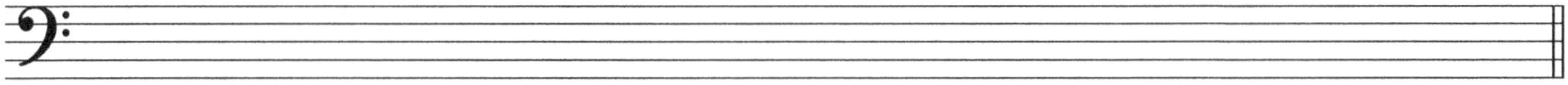

G melodic minor

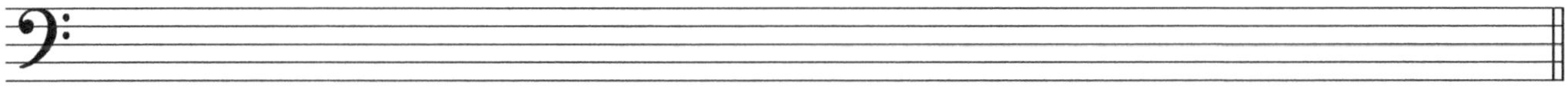

Minor Scales

6
Intervals

Interval Review

An *interval* can be defined as the distance from one note to the next. An interval is indicated by a number. There are two basic types of intervals, **harmonic** and **melodic**.

- A harmonic interval occurs when two notes are played or sung at the same time.
- A melodic interval occurs when two notes are played or sung one after the other.

Figure 6.1

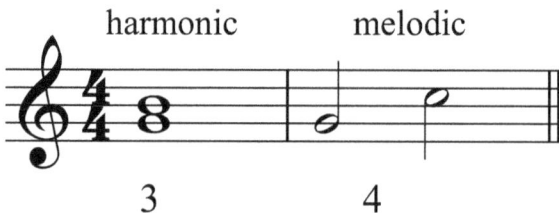

1. Write the number for the following intervals.

Intervals in Major and Minor Scales

Intervals can be built on the tonic of the major or minor scale. Figure 6.2 shows the intervals built on the tonic (G) of the G major scale. The interval of a 7th must be G-F♯ since the scale of G major has an F♯.

Figure 6.2

G major 1 2 3 4 5 6 7 8

If we write intervals on the tonic of the scale of D natural minor the 6th must contain a B♭ since B♭ is part of the D natural minor scale. Figure 6.3 shows the intervals built on the tonic of D natural minor.

Figure 6.3

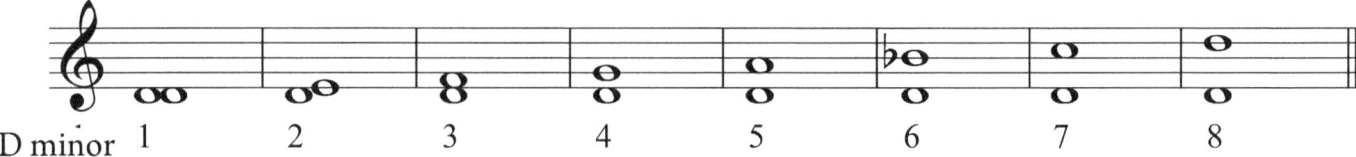

D minor 1 2 3 4 5 6 7 8

1. Write the following harmonic intervals on the tonic of the C major scale.

C major 5 8 3 4 7 6 1 2

2. Write the following harmonic intervals on the tonic of the F major scale. remember that F major has a B♭.

F major 8   4   5   3   2   1   6   7

3. Write the following melodic intervals on the tonic of the E natural minor scale. Remember that E minor has an F♯.

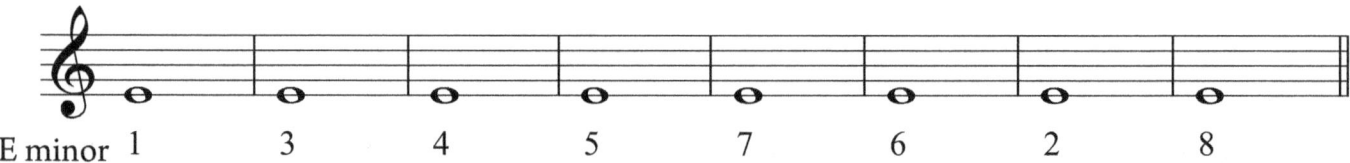

E minor 1   3   4   5   7   6   2   8

4. Write the following harmonic intervals on the tonic of the A natural minor scale.

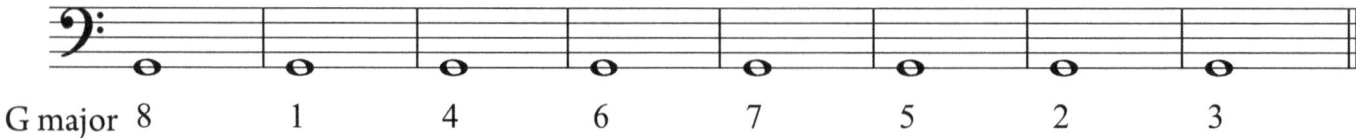

A minor 2   3   1   6   4   5   8   7

5. Write the following melodic intervals on the tonic of the G major scale.

G major 8   1   4   6   7   5   2   3

Interval Quality

As well as having a number, intervals also have a *quality*. We will begin our study with *major* and *perfect* intervals. Major and perfect are interval qualities. In order to understand how the qualities work we need to look at the major scale.

Major Intervals

The intervals that are major are: 2nds, 3rds, 6ths and 7ths. They are called major because of their sound. The symbol for a major interval is "maj" and looks like this:

maj 2   major second
maj 3   major third
maj 6   major sixth
maj 7   major seventh

In order for an interval to be major, the top note must be a member of the bottom notes scale. Figure 6.4 shows all the major intervals in D major. The major 3rd and the major 7th have sharps because in the scale of D major those two notes are sharp (F♯ and C♯). The top note of each interval belongs to the scale of D major. This is what makes them major intervals.

Figure 6.4

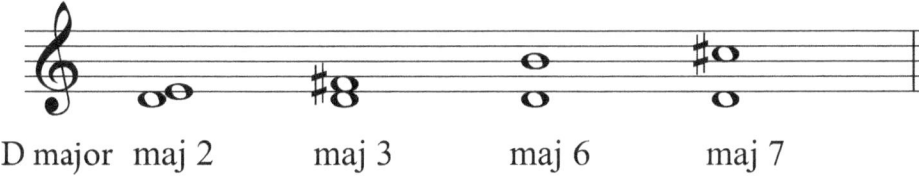

D major   maj 2   maj 3   maj 6   maj 7

Intervals

Perfect Intervals

The intervals that are perfect are: unisons (1s), 4ths, 5ths and octaves (8ths). They are called perfect because of their sound. The symbol for a perfect interval is "per" and looks like this:

per 1   perfect unison
per 4   perfect fourth
per 5   perfect fifth
per 8   perfect octave

In order for an interval to be perfect, like major, the top note must be a member of the bottom notes scale. Figure 6.5 shows all the perfect intervals in B♭ major. The top note of each interval belongs to the scale of B♭ major. This makes them perfect intervals.

Figure 6.5

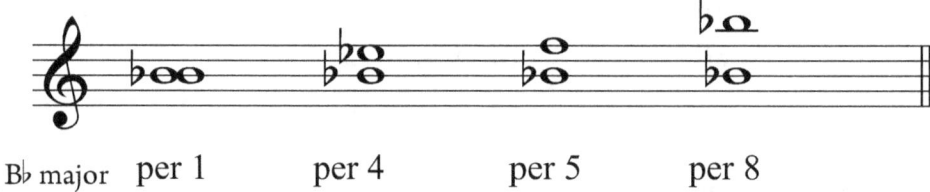

Figure 6.6 contains all the intervals in C major. The top note of each interval belongs to the C major scale. As a result of this, all of these intervals are major or perfect depending on their number.

Figure 6.6

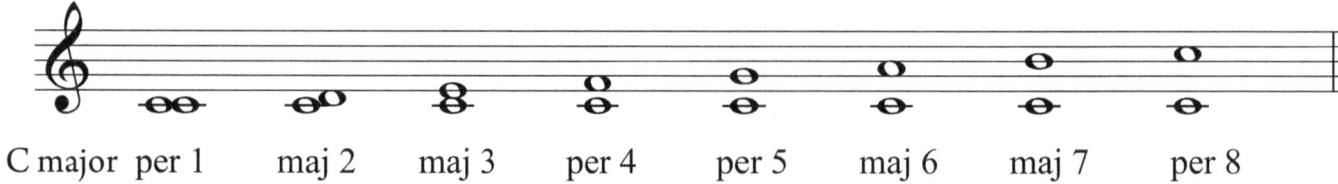

Intervals

1. Write the following intervals in the key of G major. Use accidentals instead of a key signature.

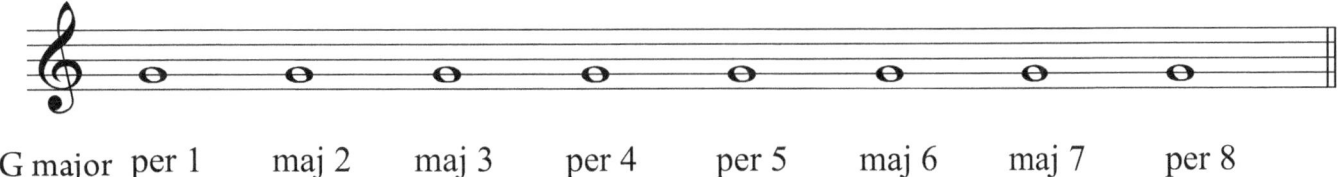

G major   per 1   maj 2   maj 3   per 4   per 5   maj 6   maj 7   per 8

2. Write the following intervals in the key of F major. Use accidentals instead of a key signature.

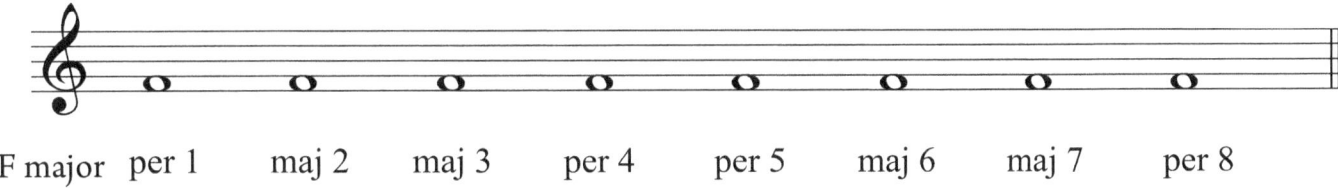

F major   per 1   maj 2   maj 3   per 4   per 5   maj 6   maj 7   per 8

3. Name the following intervals. Think of the bottom note as the tonic of a major scale.

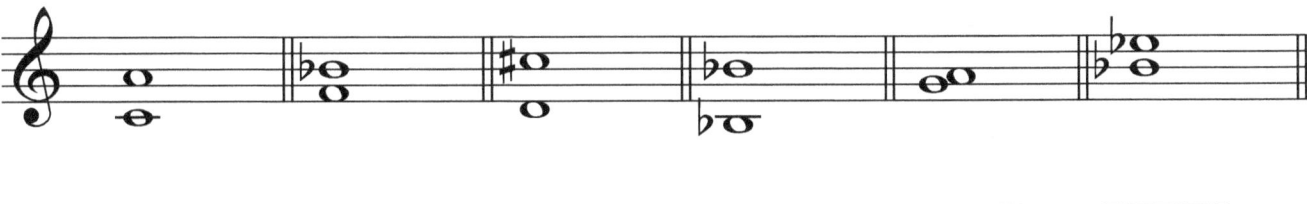

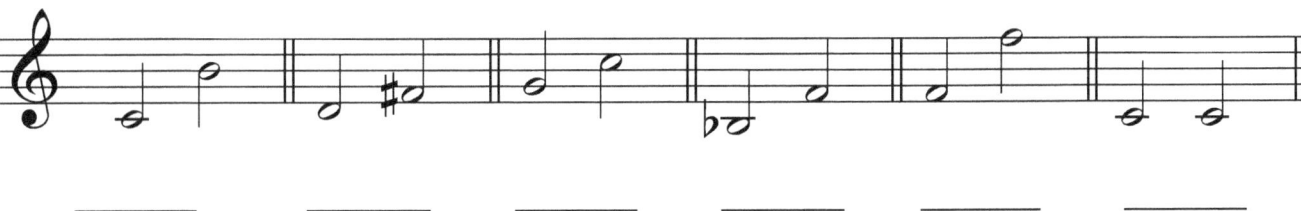

4. Write the following harmonic intervals above the given notes.

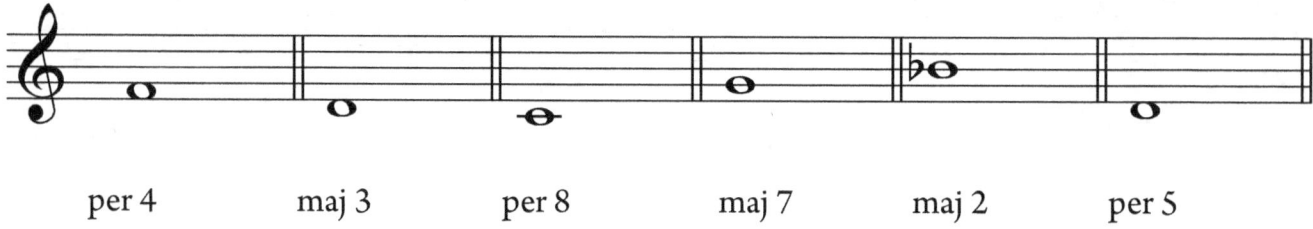

| per 4 | maj 3 | per 8 | maj 7 | maj 2 | per 5 |

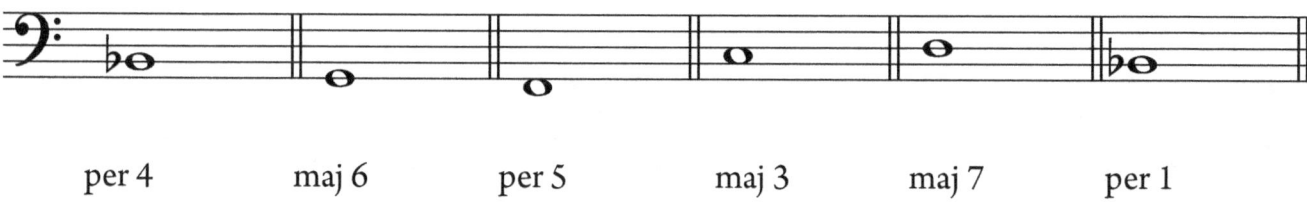

| per 4 | maj 6 | per 5 | maj 3 | maj 7 | per 1 |

5. Write the following melodic intervals above the given notes.

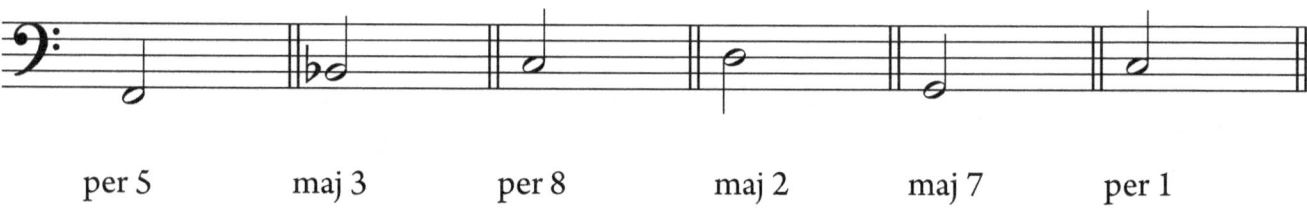

| per 5 | maj 3 | per 8 | maj 2 | maj 7 | per 1 |

| per 8 | per 8 | per 4 | maj 3 | maj 6 | maj 2 |

Intervals

Minor Intervals

When we lower the upper note of a major interval by one half step, we get a *minor interval*. Figure 6.7 contains a major 3rd and a minor 3rd in two keys. When we lower the upper note of the major 3rd by one half step we get a minor 3rd.

A major 3rd above C is E because E is the third note of the C major scale. If we lower the E to E♭, it is no longer part of the C scale and is a half step closer to C. This makes C to E♭ a minor 3rd.

A major 3rd above D is F♯ since the third note of the D major scale is F♯. In order to get a minor 3rd above D we lower the F♯ one half step to F♮.

Figure 6.7

1. Add an accidental lowering each major 3rd one half step to change it to a minor 3rd.

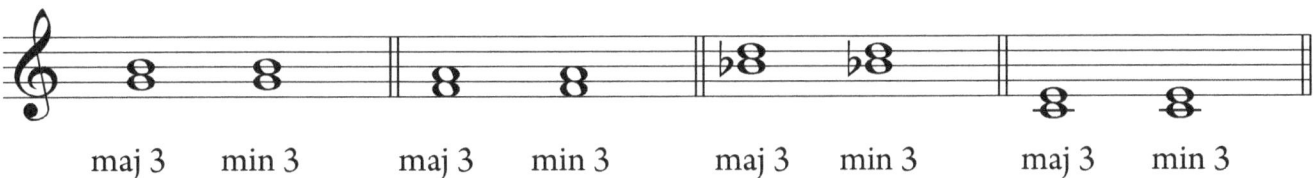

2. Name the following intervals as major 3rds or minor 3rds.

3. Write harmonic intervals above the following notes.

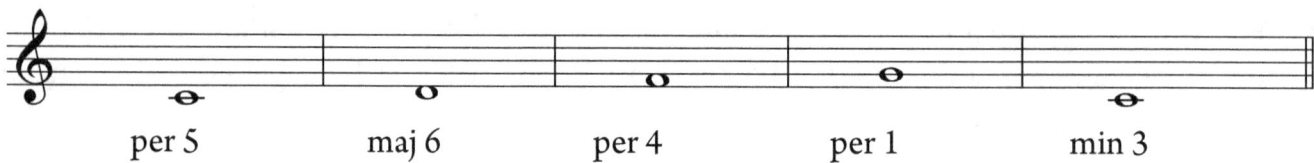

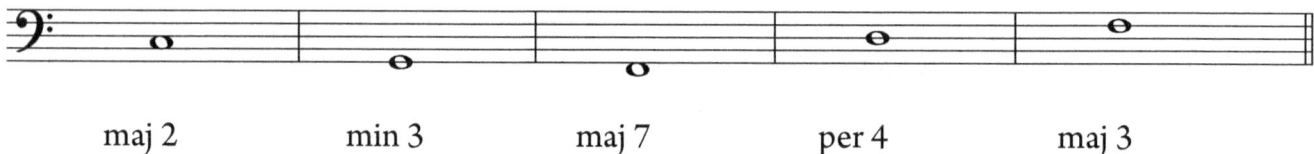

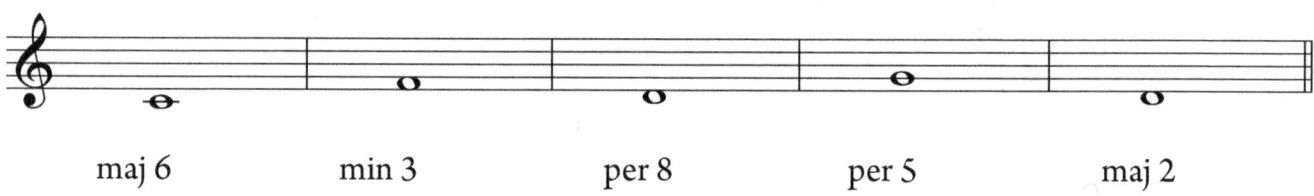

4. Name the following intervals.

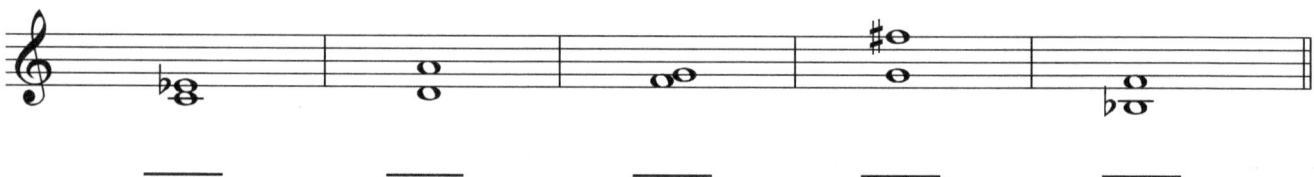

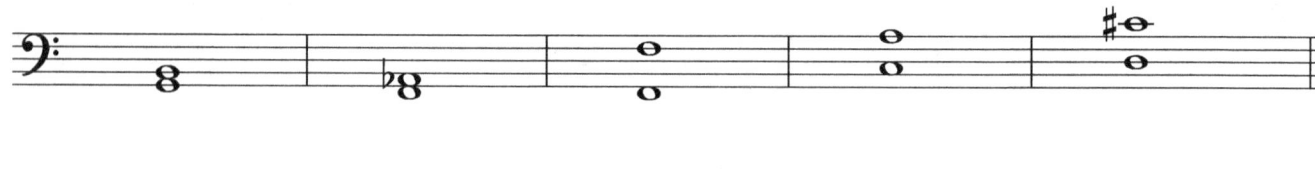

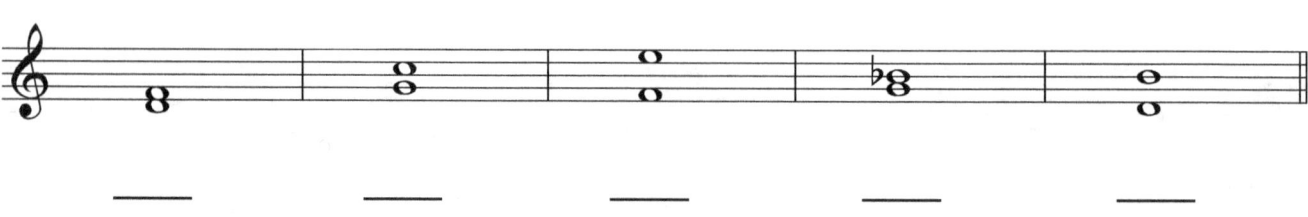

Intervals

7
Chords

Triad Review

A *chord* consists of three or more notes sounded at the same time. A *triad* is a three note chord. The *tonic triad* of any key is the triad built on $\hat{1}$ of the scale or the tonic. Figure 7.1 is the tonic triad in C major. The note that the triad is built on is called the *root*. The next note a third above it is called the *third*. The note a fifth above the root is called the *fifth*.

Figure 7.1

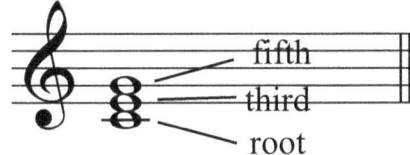

Triads in Major Keys

A triad can be built on any note of the major scale just by stacking two thirds on top of the note. In this level, we will cover triads built on $\hat{1}$ and $\hat{5}$. Scale degree $\hat{1}$ is the tonic. A triad built on the tonic of a major scale is called the *tonic triad*. Scale degree $\hat{5}$ is the dominant. A triad built on the dominant of a major scale is called the *dominant triad*. Figure 7.2 contains triads built on $\hat{1}$ and $\hat{5}$ of the C major scale. The root of the triad built on $\hat{1}$ in C major is C. The root of the triad built on $\hat{5}$ in C major is G. The root/quality chord symbols **C** and **G** are placed above the staff. The Roman numerals, called the functional chord symbols **I** and **V** are placed below the staff.

Figure 7.2

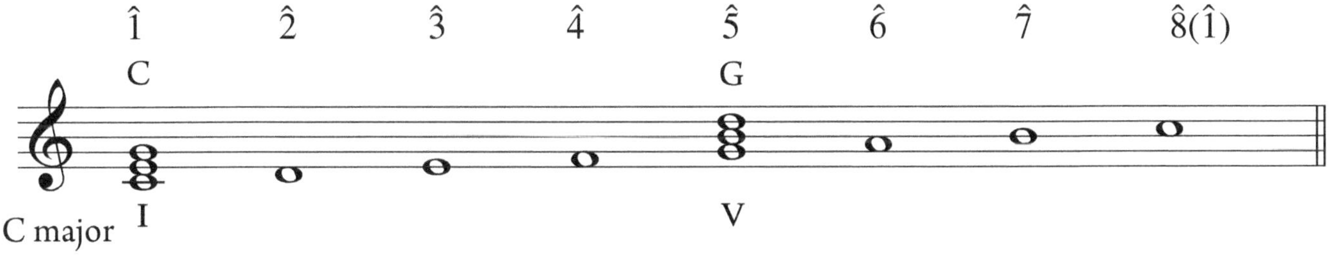

1. Name the key of the folowing scales and write triads on the tonic and dominant notes. Add Roman numeral and root/quality chord symbols for each.

key:

key:

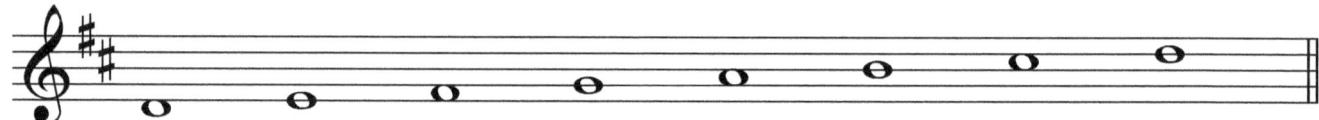

key:

key:

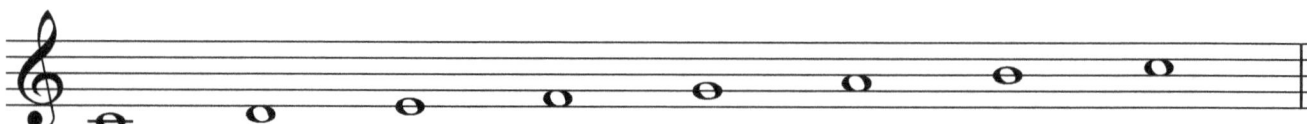

key:

2. Write the following triads using accidentals instead of a key signature. Add the functional and root/quality chords symbols for each.

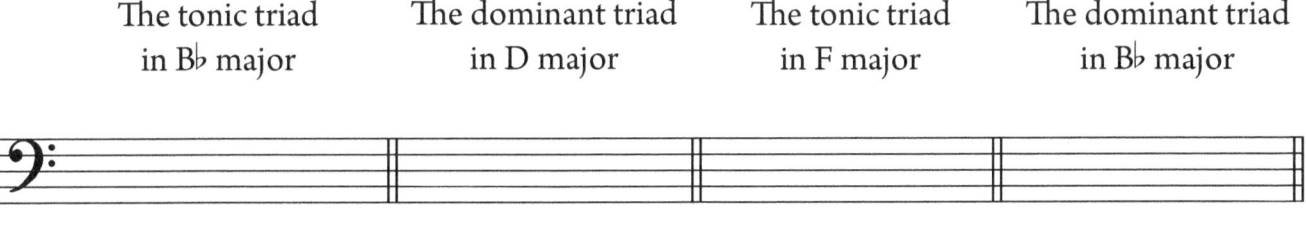

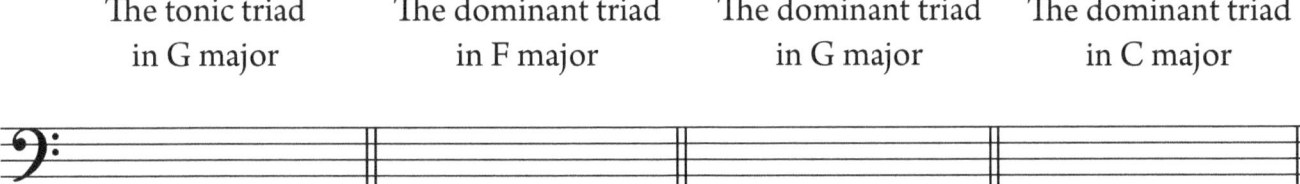

Triads in Minor Keys

Triads are also found in minor keys. Just like in major keys, we can build a triad on $\hat{1}$ or $\hat{5}$ of the harmonic minor scale to get the tonic and dominant triads in a minor key. It is important to note that the dominant triad in a minor key has raised $\hat{7}$ to reflect the harmonic form of the scale. Dominant triads in minor keys will always have an accidental for now. The third of the dominant triad is raised one half step because it is the leading tone. Figure 7.3 contains the tonic and dominant triads in A minor. The Roman numeral symbols for these chords are a lowercase "**i**" for the tonic triad and an uppercase "**V**" for the dominant triad. Raised $\hat{7}$ in A minor is G♯ and it is the third of the dominant triad. The root/quality symbol for the A minor triad is **Am**.

Figure 7.3

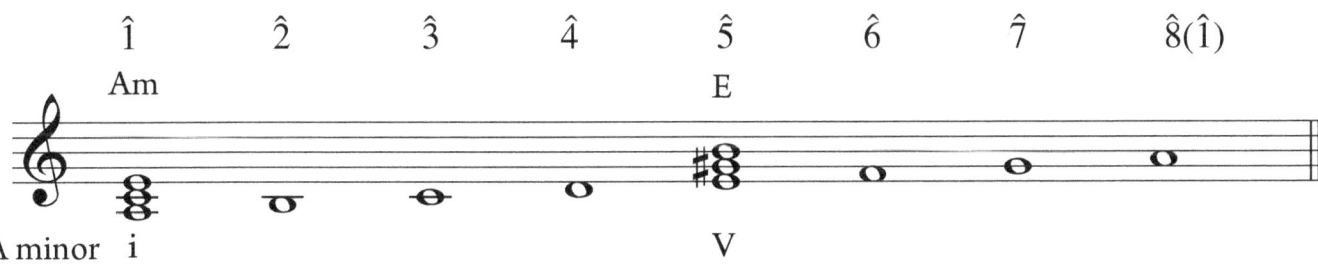

1. Name the key of the following harmonic minor scales. Write triads on the tonic and dominant notes. Add the Roman numeral and root/quality chord symbols for each.

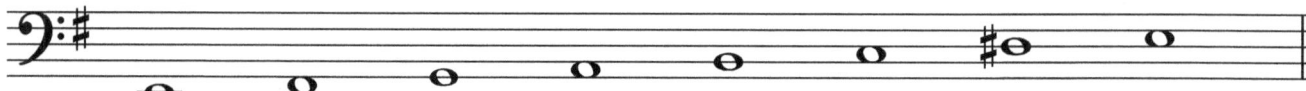

key:

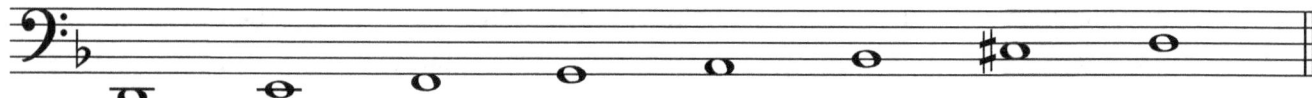

key:

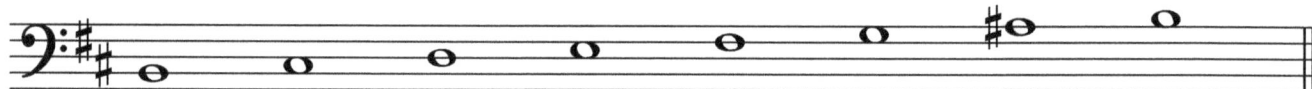

key:

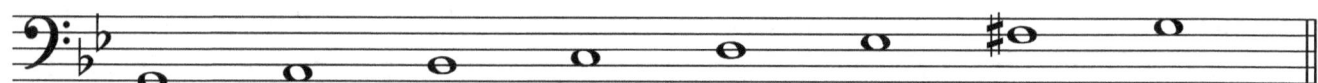

key:

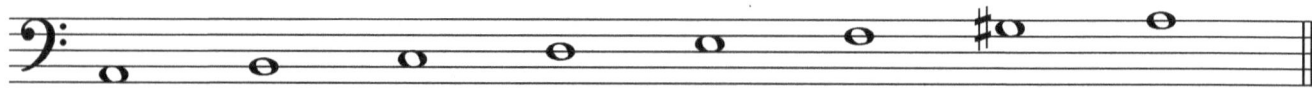

key:

2. Write the following triads using accidentals instead of a key signature. Add the Roman numeral and root/quality chords symbols for each.

| The tonic triad in A minor | The dominant triad in B minor | The tonic triad in E minor | The dominant triad in G minor |

| The tonic triad in D minor | The dominant triad in E minor | The tonic triad in G minor | The dominant triad in D minor |

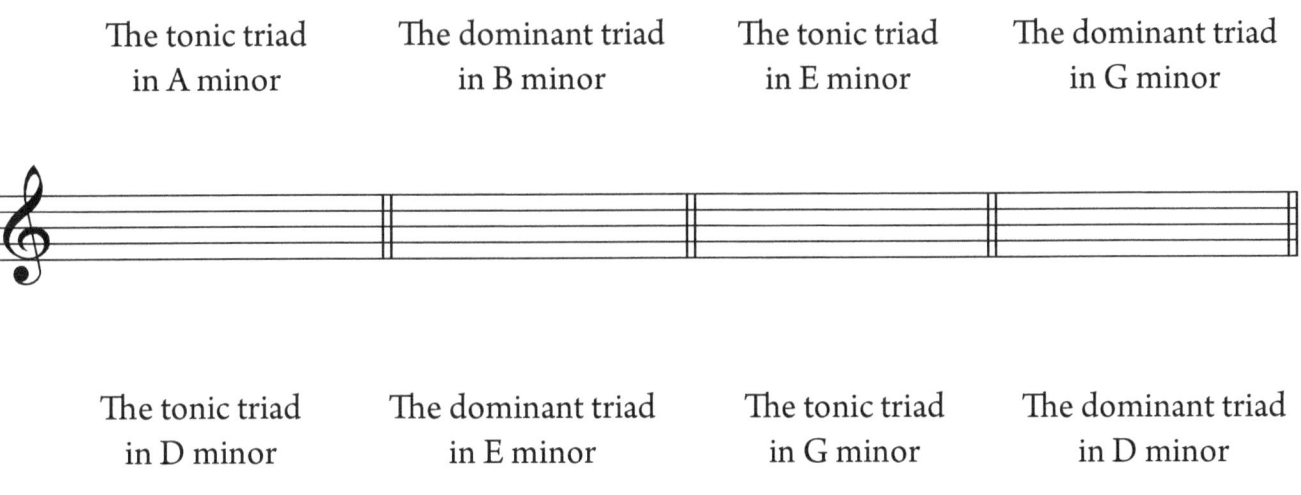

3. Name the minor key for the following. Add the chord symbol under each and label them as tonic or dominant triads.

key: key: key: key:

key: key: key: key:

Chords

8
History 2

The Anna Magdalena Bach Notebook

The *Anna Magdalena Bach Notebook* refers to two books that composer Johann Sebastian Bach gave to his second wife, Anna Magdalena on her birthday. Bach wanted Anna Magdalena to copy music of her choosing into the books. They contain keyboard music and a few pieces for voice.

One book is dated 1722, and the other is dated 1725. The better-known book is the one from 1725. It is richly decorated with gold leaf and is a beautiful book.

Anna Magdalena was a musician and singer. Most of the pieces in the book are in Anna Magdalena's handwriting, and the true identity of many of the original composers in the book is not known. There seems to be writing in the book by members of Bach's family including Carl Phillip Emmanuel Bach, and Johann Christian Bach, two of his sons. The first two pieces in the book were copied by J. S. Bach himself.

The books contain several dances, arias, chorales and other pieces of music by different composers. These composers were probably Carl Philip Emmanuel Bach, Christian Petzold, François Couperin, and other musician friends of the Bach family.

Most of these pieces were written for musical enjoyment, but also as teaching pieces for younger members of the Bach family.

Anna Magdalena loved to have musical gatherings at the Bach house where visitors were encouraged to perform and compose new pieces which were copied into the notebook.

The Harpischord

The **harpsichord,** a keyboard instrument, is an early relative of the piano. It looks a little like a grand piano but sounds much different.
The harpsichord has small hooks called quills that pluck the string when a player presses a key on the keyboard. Because of this, it is very challenging to make dynamic changes when playing the harpsichord. Since the strings are plucked, the keyboard is not touch sensitive, and the player does not have control over the volume of each note.
The pieces in the Anna Magdalena Notebook were written for a harpsichord or a similar keyboard instrument.

Music Terms

dal segno, D.S. al 𝄋   from the sign

ottava, 8va   the interval of an octave

play one octave above written pitch

play one octave below written pitch

Review 2

1. Name the following intervals.

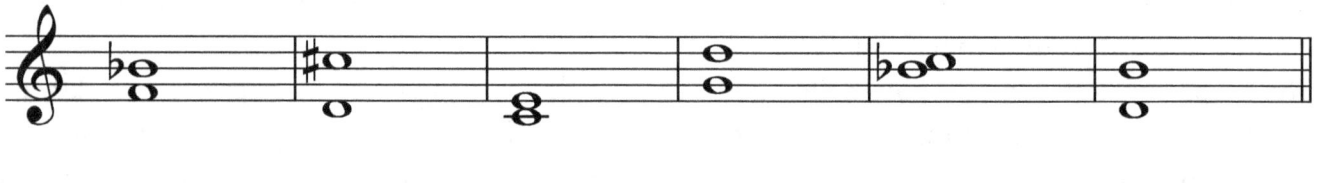

2. Write the following intervals.

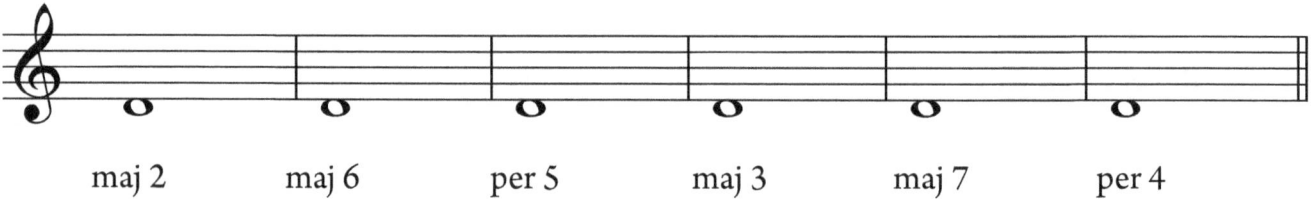

3. Write the following scales ascending and descending using a key signature for each. Use half notes.

G melodic minor

B harmonic minor

A melodic minor

D harmonic minor

E natural minor

B melodic minor

4. Write the following triads using key signatures. Place the chord symbol under each.

| The tonic triad in D major | The dominant triad in E minor | The tonic triad in B♭ major | The tonic triad in G minor |

| The tonic triad in D minor | The dominant triad in A minor | The dominant triad in F major | The dominant triad in B minor |

5. Define the following musical terms.

marcato _____

cantabile _____

maestoso _____

grazioso _____

dolce _____

ottava _____

dal segno _____

6. Rewrite the following melodies at the pitch that they are played.

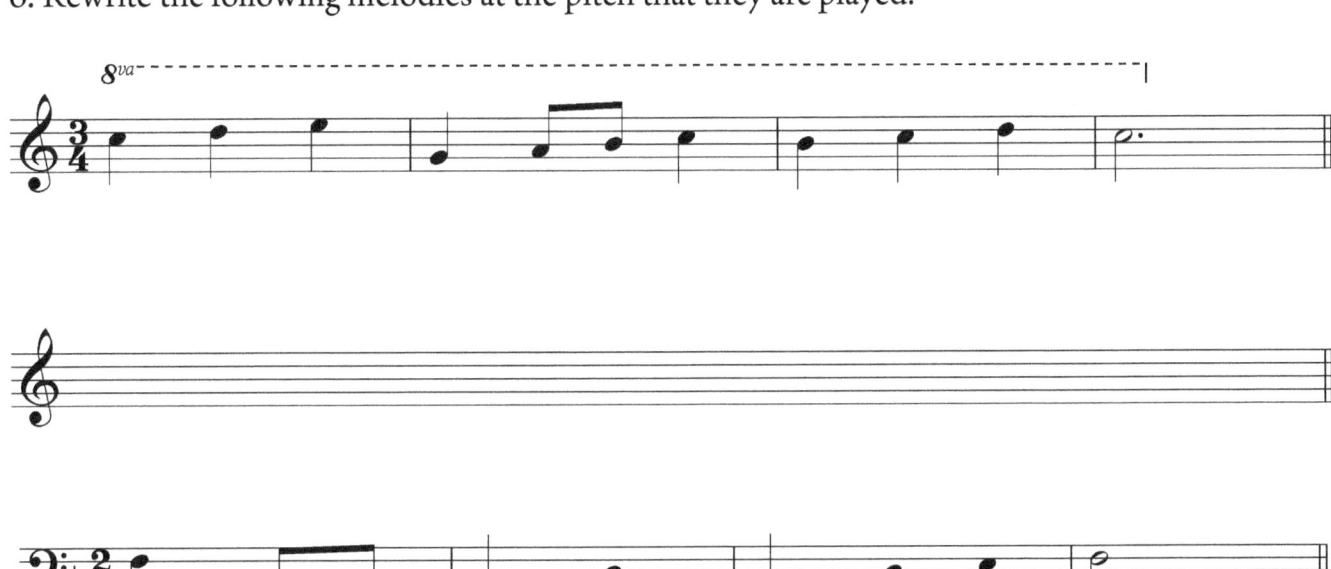

7. Answer the following questions.

a) Who created the Anna Magdalena Notebook? _____

b) Who was Anna Magdalena? _____

c) Name two composers whose music is in the Anna Magdalena Notebook.

　　1) _____

　　2) _____

d) Name three types of pieces found the the Anna Magdalena Notebook.

　　1) _____　2) _____　3) _____

e) What instrument are these pieces written for? _____

f) What type of instrument is this? _____

Review 2

9
Melody Writing

Conjunct and Disjunct Motion

Melodies move in various ways. When a melody moves by step, the motion is called ***conjunct motion***. When a melody moves by skip or leap, the motion is called ***disjunct motion***. Good melodies are a combination of both of these. Let's compare a few melodies. The melody in Figure 9.1 consists only of disjunct motion. Every note leaps and there is no stepwise motion until the last two notes. The result is a fractured melody that would be very hard to sing and to play on some instruments.

Figure 9.1

G major

The melody in Figure 9.2 contains only conjunct or stepwise motion. Although it is not a terrible melody, using only scalewise motion is not very interesting.

Figure 9.2

G major

Figure 9.3 contains a melody that is a combination of conjunct and disjunct motion. The balance of both types of motion produces an interesting melody. It should be noted that this melody is in G major and both the tonic and dominant chords are outlined within it. The tonic chord (G B D) occurs in measure one and the dominant chord (D F♯ A) can be found in measure three. These are the two most prominant chords in any key. Using these chords creates a strong melody that is clearly based on the key of G major. In this level, we are going to write melodies that use stepwise motion and skips or leaps based on the tonic and dominant triads.

Figure 9.3

G major

Stable and Unstable Scale Degrees

The most **stable** scale degree in any key is $\hat{1}$. A stable scale degree provides us with a sense of rest and completeness or finality. Many melodies begin and end on $\hat{1}$. This is the tonic, and the primary and most important note of any key. Scale degree $\hat{3}$, being the 3rd of the tonic triad is also a relatively stable degree with which to end a phrase.
Certain scale degrees like $\hat{2}$ are considered **unstable**. Unstable scale degrees are like question marks. There must be another phrase to answer a phrase that ends on an unstable degree. A phrase may end on $\hat{2}$, but it cannot be the last phrase of a piece of music. Play the phrases in Figure 9.4 and listen to the difference between a phrase that ends on $\hat{2}$ an unstable degree, and $\hat{1}$ the most stable degree.

Figure 9.4

F major

Melody Writing

Writing a Melody

The tonic and dominant chords are very strong elements to use in a melody. Figure 9.5 shows some of the ways the tonic triad in C major can be incorporated into a melody to add interest and variety with disjunct motion. Study the C major tonic triads used melodically.

    a) The tonic triad (C E G) is written into the melody creating skips of a 3rd.
    b) The skips are softened slightly with stepwise motion beween the 3rd and 5th (E F G).
    c) The stepwise motion may be placed between the root and 3rd (C D E).
    d) The triad may be outlined backwards from the 5th down to the root (G E C).

Figure 9.5

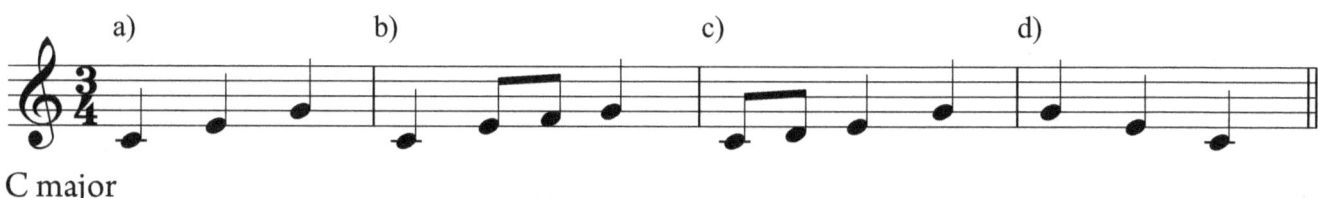

C major

The dominant triad is also effective in a melody. Since the dominant triad contains the leading tone, it is often followed by the tonic. It is very strong to end a melody on $\hat{1}$. This is the most stable tone in any key. When you end a melody on $\hat{1}$ it is often preceded by $\hat{7}$ or $\hat{2}$, both notes of the dominant triad. A strong melodic ending consists of the final two notes $\hat{2}$ - $\hat{1}$ or $\hat{7}$ - $\hat{1}$. Figure 9.6 shows two strong endings for a melody using the notes of the dominant triad. a) outlines the dominant triad in C major (G B D) and ends on the tonic ($\hat{2}$ - $\hat{1}$). b) uses the root and 3rd of the dominant triad and ends on the tonic ($\hat{7}$ - $\hat{1}$).

Figure 9.6

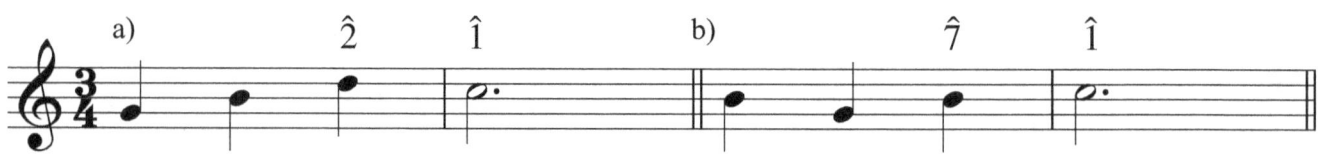

C major

Melody Writing

1. Write a melody in F major using a combination of stepwise motion and skips outlining the tonic or dominant triad. Use the rhythm provided and end on a stable pitch ($\hat{1}$ or $\hat{3}$).

2. Write a melody in D major using a combination of stepwise motion and skips outlining the tonic or dominant triad. Use the rhythm provided and end on a stable pitch ($\hat{1}$ or $\hat{3}$).

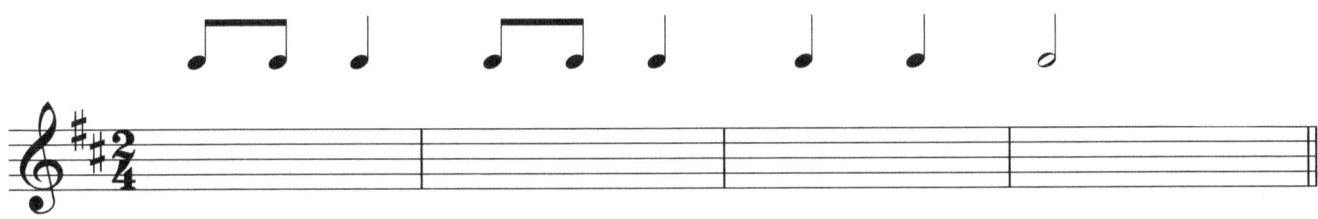

3. Write a melody in B♭ major using a combination of stepwise motion and skips outlining the tonic or dominant triad. Use the rhythm provided and end on a stable pitch ($\hat{1}$ or $\hat{3}$).

4. Write a melody in G major using a combination of stepwise motion and skips outlining the tonic or dominant triad. Use the rhythm provided and end on a stable pitch ($\hat{1}$ or $\hat{3}$).

5. Write a melody in C major using a combination of stepwise motion and skips outlining the tonic or dominant triad. Use the rhythm provided and end on a stable pitch ($\hat{1}$ or $\hat{3}$).

10
Music Analysis

Form in Melody

The overall plan or structure of a piece of music is known as *form*. We label music with letters to distinguish the differences within a composition.

Let's examine the two phrase melody in Figure 10.1. This melody is in the key of D major and begins on the stable scale degree $\hat{3}$ (F♯). The first phrase ends on the unstable degree $\hat{2}$ (E). The second phrase begins like the first and continues until the end where the last bar is slightly different, ending on the stable scale degree $\hat{1}$ (D).

We can label each phrase with a letter to indicate the form. The first phrase is labeled '**a**.' The second phrase being the same, except for the ending, is labeled '**a¹**.' This shows that the phrases are related, but there is a slight variation. If the phrases were exactly the same, they would be labeled with two '**a**'s. It should be noted that each phrase is four measures long. This is a common length for a phrase.

These two phrases together form a section called a ***parallel period***. A parallel period is formed when the two phrases are similar.

Figure 10.1

Ludwig van Beethoven
Symphony No. 9, IV

a

D major

a¹

Figure 10.2 contains a melody that is made up of two distinctly different phrases. Each phrase begins with a quarter note upbeat. This, along with the rhythm, which is the same between the two phrases, is a unifying feature. However, the phrases are still very different. The first phrase contains a melody that ascends, and the second phrase contains a melody that descends. They work well together, but are not the same. To show this difference, the first phrase is labeled '**a**' and the second phrase is labeled '**b**.'

These two phrases together form a section called a ***contrasting period***. A contrasting period occurs when the two phrases of a period are different or contrasting.

Figure 10.2

Scottish Air

F major

1. For the following melodies: name the key, mark the phrases, and label them with letters (a, a¹, b) indicating their form.

Welsh Air

key:

Music Analysis

Irish Air

key:

American Folk Tune

key:

Carol based on Chant
"O Come, O Come Emmanuel"

key:

Allegro

Alexander Reinagle
(1756 - 1809)

a. Add the correct time signature directly on the music.

b. Name the key of this piece._____

c. Name the composer of this piece. _____

d. Draw a phrase mark over each phrase.

e. Label the phrases according to the form (a, a¹, b)

f. These two phrases form a: ❏ contrasting period   ❏ parallel period

g. Does the second phrase end on a stable or unstable degree? _____

h. Define **Allegro**._____

i. How are measure 1 and 2 similar to 5 and 6? _____

j. Locate and circle a half step in this piece.

Carefree

Daniel Gottlob Turk
(1756 - 1813)

a. Add the correct time signature directly on the music.

b. Name the key of this piece._____

c. Name the composer of this piece._____

d. Draw a phrase mark over each phrase.

e. Label the phrases according to the form (a, a¹, b)

f. These two phrases form a: ☐ contrasting period ☐ parallel period

g. Does the second phrase end on a stable or unstable degree?_____

h. Define **Moderato**._____

i. Find and circle one accidental in this piece.

j. Name the interval at letter A. _____

k. Name the interval at letter B. _____

Music Analysis

Bagatelle

Anton Diabelli

a. Add the correct time signature directly on the music.

b. Name the key of this piece. _____

c. Name the composer of this piece. _____

d. Draw a phrase mark over each phrase.

e. Label the phrases according to the form (a, a¹, b)

f. Does the second phrase end on a stable or unstable degree? _____

g. Find and circle one dominant triad in this piece.

h. Name the interval at letter A. _____

i. Name the interval at letter B. _____

j. Explain the sign at letter C. _____

k. On what measure does this piece begin? _____

Music Analysis

11
History 3

The Baroque Dance

A *Baroque dance* is an instrumental dance composed during the Baroque era (1600 - 1750). Dance music was very popular in the Baroque era, and composers were often asked to write dances for parties and functions.

The Anna Magdalena Notebook contains some of these Baroque dances written for keyboard. One of the most common dances found in this notebook is the *minuet*. A minuet is a dance for two people in 3/4 time that originated in France. It may be spelled differently in different countries. In Italy, it was called the *minuetto* and in France the *menuet*. Eventually, minuets were written for non-dancing purposes and became a musical form used for keyboard pieces and movements of symphonies. Minuets can also be found in operas, ballets, and plays.

One of the most famous minuets ever written, the *Minuet in G Major*, is in the Anna Magdalena Notebook. We are not exactly sure who wrote it, but credit is given to the composer Christian Petzold. The melody from this minuet has been used in pop songs and movie themes. Figure 11.1 contains the opening eight measures of this famous minuet. Play it and see if you recognize it.

Figure 11.1

Minuet in G Major

Attributed to
Christian Petzold
BWV 114

Another common dance from the Baroque era is the ***gavotte***. The gavotte is a folk dance from France. The music for a gavotte has a four beat feel and is moderately fast. It usually starts with upbeats (or an anacrusis) on beats three and four. Gavottes written in the Baroque period were not written for dancing but as musical pieces to listen to and enjoy.

Composers began writing **Suites**, which were larger compositions consisting of six or seven short dance-based pieces. The gavotte was often one of these pieces. The best-known examples of the gavotte are found in the suites written by J.S.Bach.

The following musical excerpt is the beginning of the Gavotte from J.S. Bach's French Suite in G major, BWV 816. BWV is a catalog number given to Bach's compositions to identify them. This gavotte is the fourth dance in the suite, and it is written for harpsichord.

This dance begins with two quarter note upbeats. This is a characteristic of a gavotte. The time signature ₵ is an abbreviation for 2/2 time. The top number tells us that there are two beats in each measure and the bottom number tells us that the half note receives one beat.

In this piece, the stems in the treble clef are placed in two directions. This indicates that the right hand is playing two different melodies. One melody has the stems going up, and one melody has the stems going down. The lower melody in the treble clef in mm.3-4 has three quarter rests. Here, the bottom voice is resting. The bass clef has its own melody. Music from the Baroque period is often based on 2, 3, 4, or more melodies that all work together to create a composition. This is called ***counterpoint***.

Search the internet for a recording of this Gavotte. Try to find a performance using the harpsichord to hear how it sounds on this instrument.

Another popular dance in the Baroque suite is the *gigue*. Gigue is the French word for a lively dance in triple time. In Italian, it is called "*giga*," and in English, it is "*jig*." The gigue is often seen in the Baroque dance suite as the last piece or movement.

Gigues use time signatures like 6/8, 9/8, or 12/16. Melodies are made up of rapidly moving groups of three eighth or three sixteenth notes. Most gigues are divided into four measure phrases and are written in counterpoint, using 2, 3, or more melodies that work together.

The following excerpt is the Gigue from French Suite in G Major, BWV 816, by J.S. Bach. This piece is written for harpsichord. The gigue begins with one melody in the treble clef. A second melody starts at the end of measure 3 in the treble clef. Here, the stems go in the opposite direction to show the two different melodies. A third melody is added at the end of measure 6, in the left hand. All three of these lines work together to create a masterful piece of music.

Review 3

1. Name the following intervals.

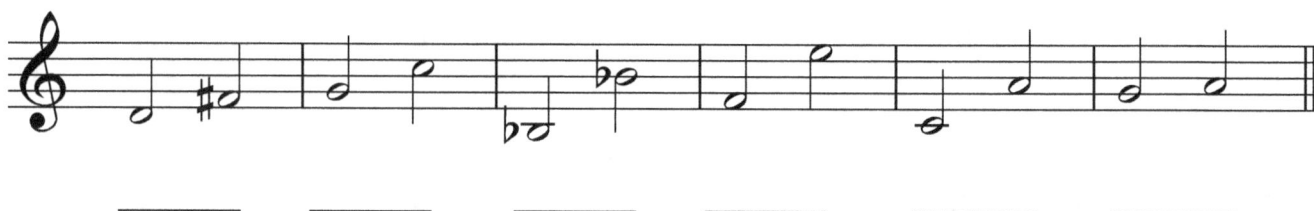

2. Add one note to complete each measure according to the time signatures.

3. Write the following scales ascending and descending in whole notes using key signatures.

A melodic minor

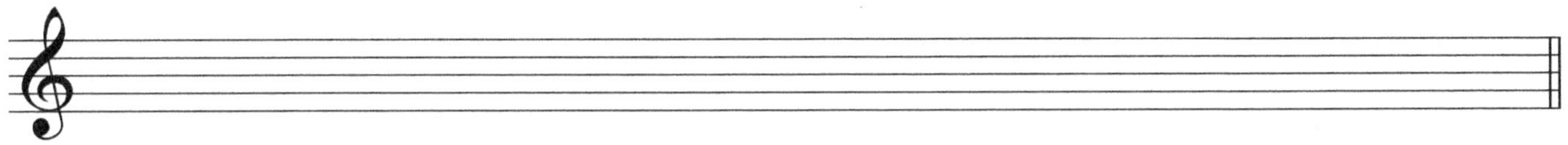

B♭ major

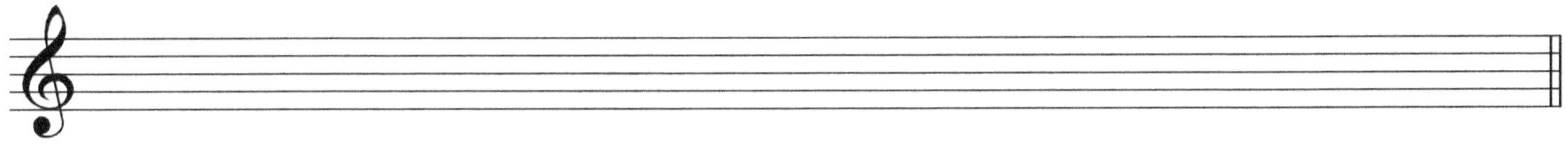

D harmonic minor

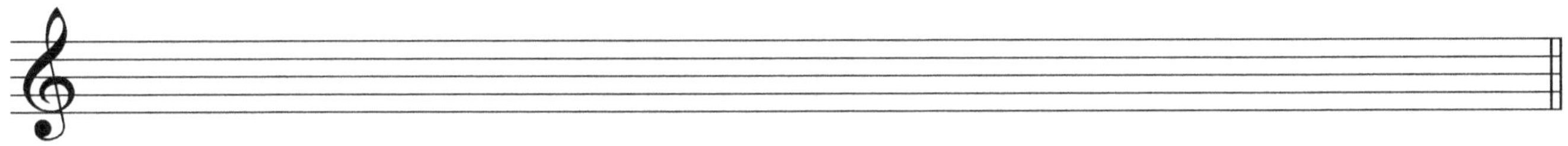

F major

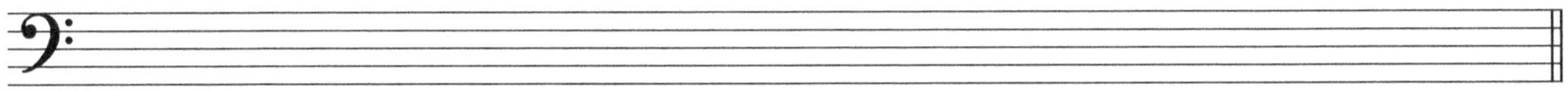

E melodic minor

D major

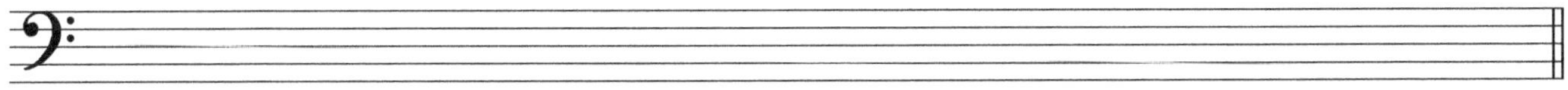

4. Write a melody in D major using a combination of stepwise motion and skips outlining the tonic or dominant triad. Use the rhythm provided and end on a stable pitch ($\hat{1}$ or $\hat{3}$).

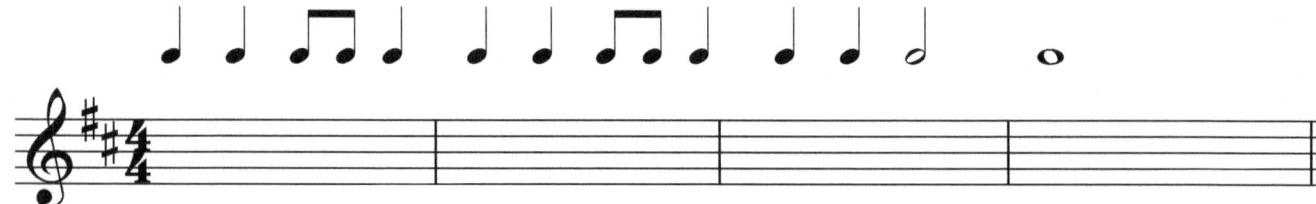

5. Write a melody in B♭ major using a combination of stepwise motion and skips outlining the tonic or dominant triad. Use the rhythm provided and end on a stable pitch ($\hat{1}$ or $\hat{3}$).

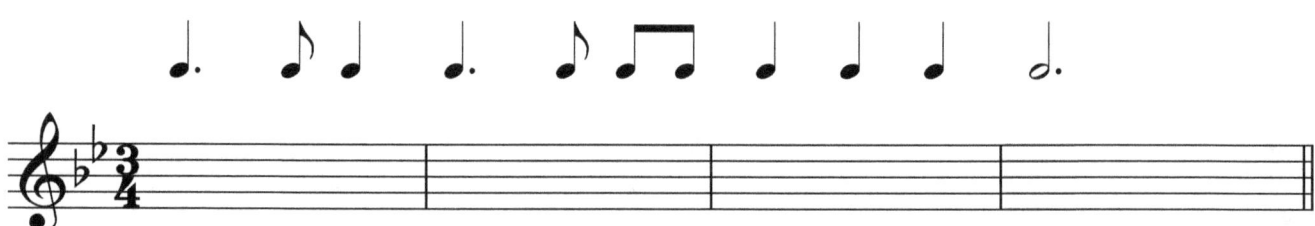

6. Give the musical terms for the following definitions.

_____	marked or stressed
_____	graceful
_____	sweet
_____	majestic
_____	in a singing style
_____	the interval of an octave
_____	from the sign

7. Answer the following questions.

a) What musical era did J.S. Bach live? _____

b) When did this era occur? _____

c) In what country was he born? _____

d) What is the Anna Magdalena Notebook? _____

e) Name two composers whose music is in the Anna Magdalena Notebook.

    1) _____

    2) _____

f) Name three types of pieces found the the Anna Magdalena Notebook.

    1) _____   2) _____   3) _____

g) What instrument are these pieces written for? _____

h) What type of instrument is this? _____

i) In what country did the minuet originate? _____

j) What is the time signature of a minuet? _____

k) In what country did the gavotte originate? _____

l) Does the gavotte begin with an anacrusis? _____

m) What is a suitable Italian term for the tempo of a gigue? _____

n) The notes of a gigue usually occur in groups of _____

o) Where does the gigue usually occur in the Baroque dance suite? _____

Music Terms and Signs

Terms

accent	a stressed note
allegretto	fairly fast, a little slower than allegro
allegro	fast
andante	moderately slow, at a walking pace
a tempo	return to the original tempo
cantabile	in a singing style
crescendo, cresc.	becoming louder
da capo, D.C.	from the beginning
D.C. al fine	repeat from the beginning and end at *Fine*
dal segno, D.S.	from the sign
decrescendo, decresc.	becoming softer
diminuendo, dim.	becoming softer
dolce	sweetly, gentle
fine	the end
forte, f	loud
fortissimo, ff	very loud
grazioso	gracefully

legato	smooth
lento	slow
maestoso	majestically
marcato	play marked or stressed
mezzo forte, mf	moderately loud
mezzo piano, mp	moderately soft
moderato	at a moderate tempo
molto	much, very
ottava, 8va	the interval of an octave
pianissimo, pp	very soft
piano, p	soft
poco	little
presto	very fast
rallentando, rall.	slowing down
ritardando, rit.	slowing down gradually
staccato	play short and detached
tempo	speed at which music is performed

Signs

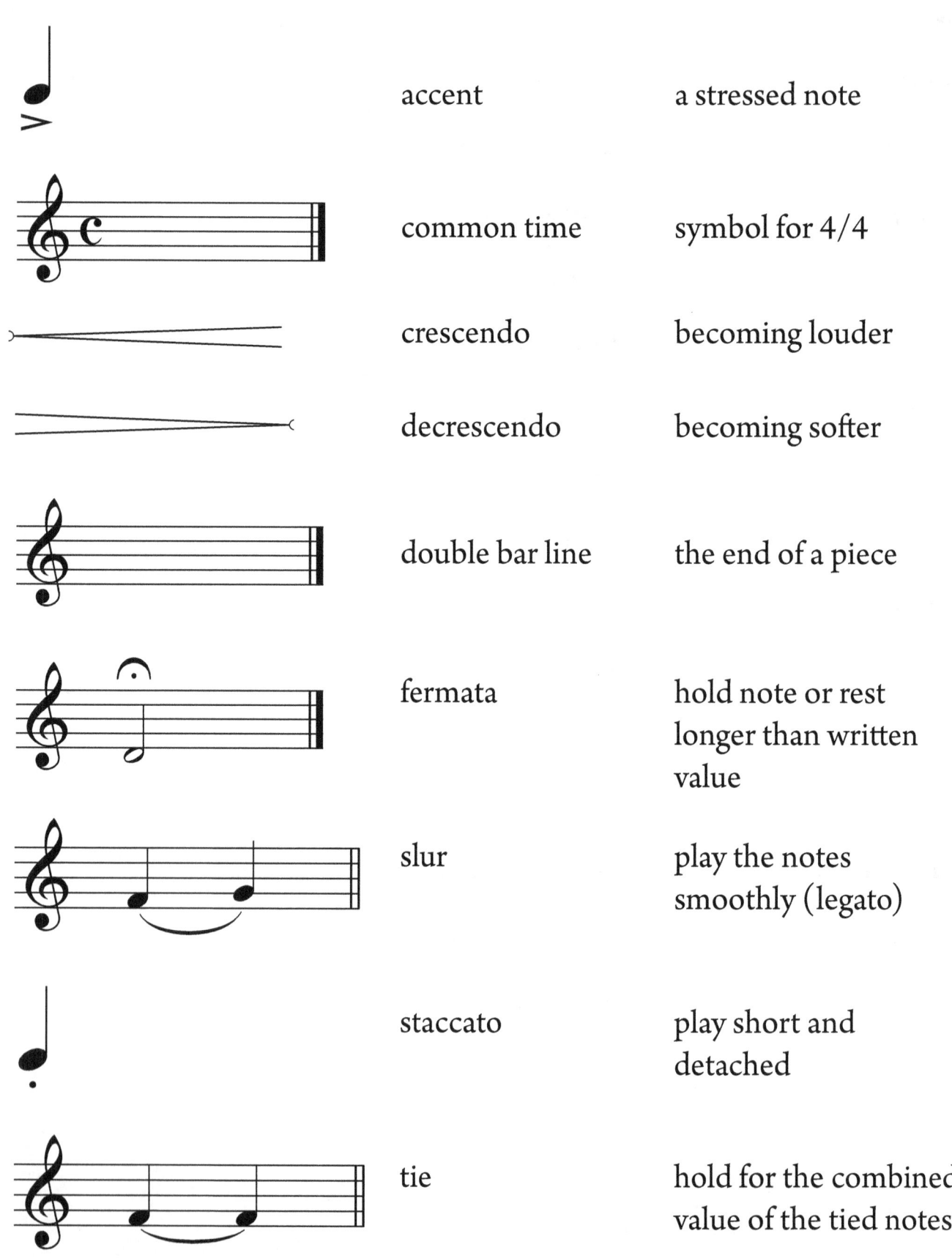

85

Terms

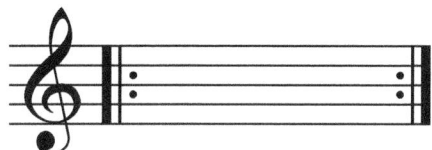 **repeat marks** - at the second sign go back to the first sign and repeat the music from there. The first sign is left out if the music is repeated from the beginning.

 **tenuto mark** - when placed over or under a note, hold it for its full value.

 **pedal symbol** - press/release the right pedal.

 **dal segno, D.S.** - from the sign.

8va - play one octave higher than written pitch.

 **8va** - play one octave lower than written pitch.

www.ingramcontent.com/pod-product-compliance
Lightning Source LLC
Chambersburg PA
CBHW081625100526
44590CB00021B/3601